You Can Be an Optimist

Be Your Best Self

You Can
Be an
Optimist

Lucy MacDonald, EdM

Rosen
YA
New York

This edition published in 2018 by
The Rosen Publishing Group, Inc.
29 East 21st Street
New York, NY 10010

Library of Congress Cataloging-in-Publication Data

Names: MacDonald, Lucy, 1953– author.
Title: You can be an optimist / Lucy MacDonald, EdM.
Description: New York, NY : Rosen Publishing, [2018] | Series: Be your best self |
Audience: Grade level: 7–10. | Includes bibliographical references and index.
Identifiers: LCCN 2017001626 | ISBN 9781508175902 (library bound book)
Subjects: LCSH: Optimism. | Happiness.
Classification: LCC BF698.35.O57 M23 2018 | DDC 149/.5—dc23
LC record available at https://lccn.loc.gov/2017001626

Manufactured in China

Photo Credits: Cover pkchai/Shutterstock.com; interior pages design NottomanV1/
Shutterstock.com

CONTENTS

INTRODUCTION

If you are naturally a skeptic, you will perhaps be doubting whether there is any point in working through this book. However, before you put it back on the shelf, ask yourself what you have to lose. Yes, you will have to invest a certain amount of time to read the book and to do the exercises. If you come out the other end feeling much the same as before, you might consider that time and money wasted.

Now, consider what you stand to gain. If, as a result of working through this book, you are able to cultivate a more positive outlook, the rewards you will reap will be huge. You will be happier, more successful, better equipped to tackle challenges, and it is likely that your health will also benefit. I can't offer any sure guarantee that this book will teach you to become an optimist, but I do know from personal experience that optimism is a behavior that can be learned. I have a confession to make. I am not an optimist, at least not by nature—my default mechanism is pessimism. My pessimistic nature is part of my genetic heritage. I have, however, learned to become optimistic, and now I am a convert to the power of optimism in my daily life.

Meeting my husband-to-be at the age of seventeen was the first time I became aware of optimism as a personality trait—he was, and is, Mr. Optimism! When I was twenty-one, he encouraged me to continue with my education and declared his confidence in my ability to achieve whatever I wanted to achieve in life. Our subsequent marriage and the parenting of four children gave me plenty of opportunities to develop my optimism skills—especially as three of my children were born within the space of four and a half years! My children have taught me more than I ever could have hoped to teach them: they taught me that by far the most important thing in my life is my family and that all the other stuff is, well, just stuff.

My next big lesson in optimism was during my college education. I returned to school full time at the age of forty, when my children were between ages eight and eighteen. By never losing sight of my goals, I maintained an optimistic attitude in the face of a daunting workload at school and at home. Those six years were a roller coaster of perseverance and hope, resulting in undergraduate and postgraduate degrees in counseling psychology. My husband and children became my cheerleaders, spurring me on when discouragement and fatigue threatened to overwhelm me. Besides my family, my education is the thing of which I am most proud, and the thrill of that accomplishment will never fade. It is a testament to what a positive attitude, combined with a tremendous amount of hard work, can accomplish.

As a counselor in private practice, I have the honor of witnessing the optimism and courage that my clients display as they struggle to deal with life's challenges.

Invariably, those who are able to find some tiny thread of positivity in difficult situations manage to hang on until the tide changes and they are able to experience happiness again. Unfortunately, the opposite is also true: those clients for whom pessimism is the default find it so much harder to recover from their troubles. Only when they develop a more optimistic outlook are they truly able to regain their balance. It is not that optimism solves all of life's problems; it is just that it can sometimes make the difference between coping and collapsing.

The process of writing this book was my latest lesson in the power of optimism. We most often teach what we need to learn. When I was approached to write a book about optimism, my spirits soared, then crashed. I felt honored one day, scared to death the next. After thinking about it, I told my husband that I was going to turn down the offer—I was not capable of completing such a task. "You can do this," he told me. "Just take it one day at a time and, before you know it, it will be done." Mr. Optimism delivers again! Throughout the writing of this book, my optimism skills, such as persistence and self-motivation, were put to good use. It would appear that I am destined to be a life-long student of optimism.

I have learned to become optimistic, and so can you. This book is designed to enable you to help set up the pillars of an optimistic attitude and to integrate optimism into your daily life. Throughout you will find a variety of exercises that allow you to practice the many aspects of optimism. Some of them are suggestions that work for me; others are based on the research of psychologists, such as Martin Seligman, who specialize in optimism. There's nothing particularly complicated about the science of optimism, but sometimes the most obvious things are the hardest to see.

My wish for you is that optimism become your constant companion—it is a fine companion indeed.

Believe in yourself! Have faith in your abilities!
Without a humble but reasonable confidence in your
own powers you can't be successful or happy.

Norman Vincent Peale (1898–1993)

WHAT IS OPTIMISM?

Optimism is a term that is familiar to us all, conveyed commonly in metaphors such as the half-full glass, the silver lining, and the sunny side of the street. However, what exactly is optimism? What comprises it?

How does it help you? Where does it come from? Can it be measured? How can you tell if you are an optimist? How can you learn to be an optimist?

In this chapter, we will answer all of these questions, drawing conclusions from the many studies conducted into optimism over the past fifty years. And we will explore the key components of optimism, such as emotional intelligence, self-esteem, resilience, and happiness.

Understanding how optimism works is the first step in your journey toward a more fulfilled, happy, and optimistic life. One thing that you will learn from this book is that there is no substitute for action. Take that first step now.

UNDERSTANDING OPTIMISM

Optimism is a positive, upbeat attitude toward the world that sets you up for success in school, relationships, career, and many other parts of life. It enables you to overcome life's difficulties—to bounce back and thrive. Daniel Goleman states in his book *Emotional Intelligence* (1995) that optimism "means having a strong expectation that, in general, things will turn out all right in life, despite setbacks and frustrations. ... optimism is an attitude that buffers people against falling into apathy, hopelessness, or depression in the face of tough going."

Martin Seligman, the father of learned optimism and author of several books on the subject, defines optimism in terms of how we explain to ourselves good and bad events using three dimensions: internal/external; permanent/temporary; and pervasive/specific. An optimist takes credit for good events [internal], believes that the positive effects will last [permanent], and that other aspects of his or her life will be affected [pervasive]. However, for bad events an optimist blames outside circumstances [external], maintains that the effects will not last [temporary], and that they are limited to this particular situation [specific]. The pessimistic explanatory style is like the photographic negative of the optimistic picture.

According to Seligman, your explanatory style is founded on your sense of self. If you believe you are worthwhile and deserving of happiness, your view of the world around you and events that affect you will be positive. Your perception of yourself and your abilities affects how you behave in a variety of situations. For example, if you get a bad grade on a test, the way you rationalize this setback will influence your subsequent demeanor at school and the likelihood of your future success.

An optimistic person might explain the situation in a variety of ways: "I didn't know all the facts required to get a better grade. I can try a new way to study and improve my skills and then I'll have a better chance next time." Or "That's not my strongest subject, but my skills still have value. I'll be sure to ace the test in the subject that's a better fit for me." Optimistic people approach situations with confidence and persistence because they have an expectation of success.

Pessimists take a different view—they are likely to explain why they did not get the job promotion by being critical of themselves: "I didn't the promotion I wanted because I'm not good enough. I'll never be good enough. No one will ever want the skills that I have, and there's nothing I can do about it." Pessimists are more likely to blame themselves when things go wrong and give up more easily when they encounter obstacles.

Optimism has its roots in childhood. Everyone is born with a basic temperament, which is a building block of personality. Jerome Kagan, professor of psychology at Harvard University, divides temperament into four broad types: timid, bold, upbeat, and melancholy. Your natural-born temperament is then influenced by your environment, including your family, your schooling, and your peers. This results in your characteristic pattern of feeling and acting across all the situations that you face in your life.

The good news is that your genetic heritage can be consciously overridden. For example, in Kagan's research, children with a timid temperament were able to learn to overcome their shyness by the time they reached adolescence, particularly if their parents gently encouraged them to be more outgoing. Similarly, it follows that it is possible to outgrow a melancholic temperament and learn to become more upbeat and optimistic.

One technique to achieve this goal is to pay attention to what you are thinking and interrupt any negative thoughts you might have. Find a way of reframing the negative thought in a positive way. For example, you might try interrupting the statement "I should quit playing golf because I'm not very good" with "I can enjoy golf without playing a perfect game." The key characteristics of an optimist, such as cheerfulness and persistence, are not difficult to identify. All you have to do is spend some time with a person and see how they interact with the people around them. However, you can also use a scientifically valid measure to determine a person's level of optimism. For example, Martin Seligman developed the Attributional Style Questionnaire, which gives you a score according to how optimistically or pessimistically you explain the good and bad events that you face in your life. Optimism is such a powerful tool because it gives you the confidence to handle both positive and negative events. It enables you to approach situations with assurance, persistence, and an expectation of success. Being optimistic means that you have a natural aptitude for happiness, that you can manage your perspective, and that you take an active role in creating the life you want.

PORTRAIT OF AN OPTIMIST

Many portrait artists study anatomy, on the basis that it is only by understanding the internal structure of the human body that they feel able to convey their subjects' appearance convincingly. Similarly, in order to present a rounded portrait of an optimist, it is necessary to appreciate how the inner workings of the optimist's mind influence his or her external characteristics. When attempting to define and understand the traits that distinguish the optimist, it soon becomes clear that every one of them stems directly or indirectly from the optimistic explanatory style.

To recap: optimists take credit for good events and believe that the effects will last a long time and touch other aspects of their lives, whereas they disassociate themselves from bad events, all of which they consider to be fleeting and localized. Because they believe that they are responsible for their triumphs and blameless for the setbacks they encounter, optimists keep their self-esteem at a healthy level. When people have confidence in their abilities, they develop a sense of control. Operating with the feeling of being in control makes optimists happier and less likely to suffer from anxiety, stress, and depression than those who consider themselves powerless to change their situation for the better.

Believing they have what's required to succeed, optimists are willing to take action in order to achieve their goals, which increases the possibility that they will get what they want. If it doesn't work out, they try again because their attitude is that failure is not due to their lack of ability, but to external circumstances, and so can be overcome if the circumstances change.

Experiencing success in one activity gives optimistic people the confidence to face new challenges in the expectation of further success. By being open to new fields of activity in this way, optimists continue to enrich their lives with positive experiences, which add to their feelings of happiness and fulfillment. Optimists thrive on dealing with other people, and because they tend to be involved in so many different activities, they have ample opportunity to do so. Their well-developed sense of control extends to their emotions, which they manage intelligently in order to keep their interactions positive, friendly, and productive.

On the following pages, we will examine in more detail some of the key components that contribute to an optimistic outlook, such as emotional intelligence, self-esteem, and resilience. Don't be discouraged if you feel that this portrait bears little or no resemblance to you. We have located the source of optimism: everything stems from your explanatory style, and you will soon discover that it is in your power to make your explanatory style optimistic.

EMOTIONAL INTELLIGENCE

The traditional view of intelligence is as a set of verbal, numerical, and logical skills that are measurable by means such as school exams and IQ tests. A high IQ may enable you to flourish academically, but by itself it will not help you to form productive relationships with a partner, family members, friends, colleagues, and yourself—all of which provide a platform for an optimistic, fulfilled life.

In the 1990s, psychologists Peter Salovey and John Mayer and, a few years later, Daniel Goleman, recognized that our ability to manage our emotions strongly affected our level of achievement in all walks of life. They used the term "emotional intelligence" to encompass a set of social and emotional skills, such as self-awareness, self-motivation, self-regulation, and empathy. Not only is there far more room to develop the abilities that make up emotional intelligence than those that form IQ, but the benefits of doing so are far greater.

- **Self-awareness** is the ability to recognize your feelings and to understand how they guide you. By being aware of your emotions, you minimize the risk of conflict with others and maximize the chances of resolving it if it does occur. To increase self-awareness get into the habit of stepping back to ask yourself what you are feeling and why you might be feeling that way.

- **Self-motivation** involves being able to take action to reach a goal. Optimism plays a crucial role in self-motivation: if you expect to succeed in reaching your goal, you are more likely to be motivated to set off in pursuit of it. Improve your motivation through visualization—picture yourself achieving your target and imagine how it will feel when you do.

- **Self-regulation** is the ability to manage disruptive emotions such as anger, fear, and despair. For example, if you are able to rein in your distress at seeing a coworker land the assignment you wanted, you will avoid damaging your relationship with that person. The key to self-regulation is to take time to examine your thinking so that you are able to identify and reframe negative feelings through cool-headed analysis.

- **Empathy**, the ability to understand what another person is feeling in a given situation, is the fundamental social skill. Empathy develops out of self-awareness: as we learn to recognize our own emotions we are better able to recognize emotions in others. Improve your empathy by observing both people you know and figures in the news, asking yourself "What must it be like to live through that experience?"

Emotional intelligence is the capacity for recognizing our own feelings and those of others, for motivating ourselves, and for managing emotions well in ourselves and others.

Daniel Goleman (1946–)

SELF-ESTEEM

Self-esteem is one of the most empowering qualities that you can possess, and the lack of it can be debilitating— "like driving through life with your hand-brake on," as the motivational expert Maxwell Maltz observed. With a high level of self-esteem, you'll feel able to meet life's challenges and worthy of success. As the word suggests, self-esteem is a total assessment of the value that you attach to yourself, based on your perceptions of yourself. If you consider yourself unworthy of success, you will not be able to appreciate it if it comes your way.

Not surprisingly, low self-esteem is linked to pessimism, depression, and anxiety. On the other hand, high self-esteem is associated closely with optimism. Optimists increase their self-esteem by taking personal credit for their achievements, which means that they feel deserving of their success, and they protect themselves from low self-esteem by blaming setbacks on external factors. The first step in your quest to feel good about yourself is self-acceptance—choosing to love and accept yourself unconditionally. It's not a question of deluding yourself—for example, if you've never played tennis, it would be foolish to tell yourself that you could beat the best player in the world. True self-esteem comes from making an informed evaluation and celebrating who you are. People with low self-esteem often have a distorted picture of who they are, tending to overlook their strengths and inflate their weaknesses.

RESILIENCE

For many years, research has focused on the impact of early childhood experience on adult life. According to conventional wisdom, children who suffer trauma are destined to be unhappy as adults, but does this have to be the case? Although upbringing and genetics play a part in determining your temperament, research tells us that you can triumph over your past.

In 1955, on the Hawaiian island of Kauai, Emmy Werner began a study of children who had experienced stress during infancy, perhaps as a result of poverty or family conflict. As adults, two-thirds of the group conformed to the stereotype, falling into crime or developing mental problems. However, the other third became competent, confident, caring adults. According to Werner, what made the difference was a trait called resilience. Resilience is the ability to grow and develop in

WHO DO YOU THINK YOU ARE?

The following activity helps you to evaluate yourself in a balanced way. Draw a large circle and divide it into five pie sections, one for each of the main components of your self-concept: social, physical, emotional, work, and spiritual. List your strengths and weaknesses in each section.

- The social self refers to how you relate to people. For example, do you have friends? Are you helpful? Do you enjoy company?
- In the physical section, write how you feel about your appearance, health, and fitness.
- The emotional section relates to your psychological well-being. Do you readily express your emotions? Can you manage/control them?
- For the work component, list the talents that have contributed to your achievements at work or school. Are there any weaknesses that may be hampering you?
- In the spiritual component, consider whether there is a guiding purpose to your life.

Review your lists and ask yourself how each strength and weakness shapes your self-esteem. If your list contains many more weaknesses than strengths, question each one, looking for concrete evidence. List some ways to change your weaknesses into strengths. For example, come up with an exercise routine to deal with a lack of fitness.

the face of adversity. Apart from optimism, which is an essential element of resilience, psychologists have identified a number of qualities that help us to overcome setbacks. These include high self-esteem, problem-solving skills, sociability, a sense of humor, and the ability both to create emotional distance from destructive relationships and to sustain supportive relationships.

These traits come more naturally to some people than to others, but—as we will see elsewhere in this book —we can all learn to develop them in ourselves. The life and work of psychiatrist Victor Frankl offer an inspiring example of resilience in theory and in action. After being sent to Auschwitz during the Holocaust, a period in which his wife, his parents, and other family members were killed, Frankl went on to develop logotherapy, a form of existential psychology that suggests that we can gain meaning and purpose from all our experiences—even the most traumatic. He also wrote thirty-two books, including the famed *Man's Search for Meaning* (1963). He encapsulated his philosophy in this statement: "Everything can be taken from a man but the last of the human freedoms—to choose one's attitude in any given set of circumstances, to choose one's own way."

I like the dreams of the future better than the history of the past.

Thomas Jefferson, (1743–1826)

HAPPINESS

Happiness goes hand in hand with optimism. If we can learn to view all that happens to us—both good and bad events—in a positive light, we will tend to be happy. And if we are happy, we will tend to see things positively.

Because happiness can cover so many different degrees of emotion, from contentment to ecstasy, and because it may mean something different to each of us, it defies objective definition and measurement. Therefore, social scientists have turned to the concept of subjective well-being. This involves the individual defining his or her own current level of well-being by reporting in one's own terms how happy one feels and how satisfied one is with one's life. Put simply, well-being entails experiencing a pleasant mood and emotions more often than an unpleasant mood and emotions.

There is a genetic tendency that influences your ability to be happy. We know this because studies of twins have demonstrated that identical twins raised apart are more similar to each other in their happiness levels than are fraternal twins who are raised together. However, it is by no means just a question of chromosomes. Environment and circumstances also play an important part in determining well-being. For example, if you are unemployed you are less likely to be happy, regardless of your genetic inheritance. It would seem to be that the lack of meaningful activity that unemployment typically

HOW SATISFIED ARE YOU WITH YOUR LIFE?

Devised by Ed Diener, this questionnaire allows you to judge your subjective well-being. Use the seven-point scale to show how much you identify with each of the statements below. Be honest and instinctive in your responses—the whole exercise should take about a minute.

1 = strongly disagree; 2 = disagree, 3 = slightly disagree
4 = neither agree nor disagree,
5 = slightly agree; 6 = agree; 7 = strongly agree

- ○ In most ways my life is close to my ideal.
- ○ The conditions of my life are excellent.
- ○ I am satisfied with life.
- ○ So far I have got the important things I want in life.
- ○ If I could live my life over, I would change almost nothing.

As a rough indication, a score of between five and fifteen suggests a below average level of satisfaction with your life; sixteen to twenty-five is average; more than twenty-five is above average.

involves—rather than the lack of money—that accounts for its harmful effect on morale. Once we can afford the basic physical needs of life, such as food, clothing, and shelter, any additional wealth makes very little difference to our level of subjective well-being. Far more influential are factors such as self-esteem, satisfying relationships with a partner, family, and friends (for example, people in couples tend to be happier than single, widowed, or divorced people), a feeling of control over one's life and involvement in fulfilling activities. Happiness is an elusive state, and there will inevitably be times when we feel unhappy. However, there are many things we can do to create the conditions for happiness. Here are just a few suggestions:

Count your blessings: if you feel unhappy, remind yourself of the things in your life that you have to be grateful for.

Act happy: smile at yourself whenever you look in the mirror, or take five minutes now and then to remind yourself of a funny situation. Your attitude follows your behavior.

Sow your social seeds: join a club, go to church, take up a team sport. Find ways to involve yourself in situations in which you can meet people and develop close, meaningful relationships.

Follow your dreams: by setting and pursuing goals related to your interests and values, you will give yourself a sense of purpose. Achieving these goals will do wonders for your self-esteem.

COPING WITH GRIEF AND SADNESS

When faced with a traumatic event, such as the death of a loved one, a serious illness or injury, unemployment or divorce, we experience grief in reaction to our loss. Although each of us grieves differently, we commonly have to deal with a combination of powerful and painful emotions, such as anguish, distress, anger, shock, confusion, despair, and guilt. At such times, when our sense of well-being is under its greatest threat, an optimistic outlook is particularly valuable. Optimism can't help you to avoid the feelings associated with loss.

Accepting and expressing your emotions is a healthy, normal approach to grief. What optimism can do is help you draw something positive from the experience. One study of people mourning the death of a loved one found that those who were able to find a positive aspect to their grief were better able to cope with it and were even able to grow as a result of it.

For example, some people make important discoveries about themselves, such as "I am stronger than I thought I was" or "I appreciate my friends so much more than I used to." Others find comfort in the fact that they were able to say good-bye to their loved one before his or her death or learn to cherish their happy memories of their loved one.

Do work you enjoy: seek a job that is interesting and challenging. Work helps to define you—if you are happy in your work, chances are it will have a positive impact on the rest of your life. Enjoyable work increases your sense of control and self-esteem.

HOW OPTIMISTIC ARE YOU?

As you have been reading this book, you will probably have begun to ask yourself how you measure up as an optimist. Perhaps you have been thinking back to recent events—good or bad—and recalling how you reacted to them. While this is a valuable approach (and one that we will be developing later in this chapter), there are also a number of tests that psychologists have devised in order to give a scientific measure of your optimism.

Martin Seligman's pioneering work on optimism produced the Attributional Style Questionnaire, a comprehensive, detailed test to measure explanatory style. It was originally used—with some success—to predict the suitability of prospective life-insurance salespeople. Below, you will find another widely used optimism test, the Life-Orientation Test, created by Michael Scheier and Charles Carver specifically to measure dispositional optimism, which is the tendency to believe that, over time, you will generally experience good things rather than bad.

Take a few minutes to do the test. If your score indicates that you are on the optimistic side, there are plenty of ideas in this book to help you maintain your positive attitude. However, if you are at the pessimistic end of the scale, don't despair. Knowledge is power: now that you know where you stand you can take the next important step toward becoming an optimist.

THE LIFE-ORIENTATION TEST

Choose between the following options to respond to the statements below: A = *agree a lot*; B = *agree a little*; C = *neither agree nor disagree*; D = *disagree a little*; E = *disagree a lot*. Please be as honest and accurate as you can throughout. Try not to let your response to one statement influence your responses to other statements. There are no "correct" or "incorrect" answers. Answer according to your own feelings, rather than how you think "most people" would answer.

1. In uncertain times, I usually expect the best.

2. It's easy for me to relax.

3. If something can go wrong for me, it will.

4. I'm always optimistic about my future.

5. I enjoy my friends a lot.

6. It's important for me to keep busy.

7. I hardly ever expect things to go my way.

8. I don't get upset too easily.

9. I rarely count on good things happening to me.

10. Overall, I expect more good things to happen to me than bad.

For statements 1, 4, and 10: A = 4 points; B = 3 points; C = 2 points; D = 1 point; E = 0.

For statements 3, 7, and 9: A = 0; B = 1 point; C = 2 points; D = 3 points; E = 4 points.

Add both subtotals to arrive at your overall score (your responses to statements 2, 5, 6, and 8 do not count toward your score). Plot your score on the optimism scale below:

0	**6**	**12**	**18**	**24**
extreme pessimism		neutral extreme		optimism

CAN OPTIMISM BE LEARNED?

You may be wondering how we can be so sure that it is possible to learn to be an optimist. Paradoxically, the evidence that optimism can be learned stems from studies that show that pessimism can be learned. In experiments conducted by Martin Seligman in the 1960s, dogs were exposed to mild electric shocks from which they could not escape. After trying to evade the shocks without success, the dogs gave up. In the next stage, when the same dogs were given a means of escaping the electric shocks, they did not even begin to try—they had been conditioned to believe that their efforts were useless, a state of mind that Seligman dubbed "learned helplessness."

Seligman (with Donald Hiroto) later conducted a similar experiment using human volunteers. They subjected the people to inescapable noise, then gave them the opportunity to leave. The subjects reacted in the same way the dogs had—with passive resignation to the situation. Seligman and his coresearchers drew a parallel between the thought processes of learned helplessness and those that inform a pessimistic explanatory style— "it's my fault; things will never get better; this will affect everything in my life."

If a person suffers a series of setbacks that he or she feels powerless to prevent, the person may develop learned helplessness, leading to loss of motivation, reduced self-confidence, and a pessimistic belief that it does not matter what he or she tries, it will never succeed. Unless something happens to break this pattern of thinking, such an individual may develop depression.

Having shown that you can develop pessimistic thinking habits, Seligman set out to prove that it is equally possible to learn to think optimistically. With his team of researchers at the University of Pennsylvania, Seligman formulated a treatment program for children who were showing symptoms of depression or who came from troubled homes (a key risk factor for depression). The Penn Prevention Program taught the children techniques for facing difficult situations with optimism. After completing the prevention program, a number of children in the group experiencing strong depression found that their symptoms had been reduced by 35 percent. Two years later, none of the children was experiencing strong depressive symptoms! The Penn Prevention Program not only prevented the children from becoming depressed or arrested the onset of their depression, but it also made them more optimistic than their peers who had not participated in the program. Based on the Penn Prevention Program, here are four techniques to enable you to think more optimistically.

Thought catching: learn to identify the self-defeating thoughts that automatically run through your mind when you are feeling sad, depressed, or stressed.

Thought evaluation: by scrutinizing your negative thoughts, you will be able to pick out any inaccurate suppositions and generalizations upon which they are based.

Accurate explanation: replace your negative and inaccurate suppositions with more positive, realistic ones.

Decatastrophizing: instead of paralyzing yourself with thoughts about all the things that could go wrong, focus on solving the problem at hand.

Taking as an example the scenario of preparing to play in a concert, the following passage of self-talk shows how these four techniques can work together:

"I'll never be able to learn this piece for the concert—I'm just not good enough. Hold on [thought catching], how can I possibly know I'm not up to it if I don't try [thought evaluation]? This piece is no more difficult than the one I played well in last year's concert. I'll be fine if I practice [accurate explanation]. If I set aside enough time for practice now, I won't run into problems later [decatastrophizing]."

MAKE YOUR SELF-TALK POSITIVE

Your most important conversations are the ones you conduct with yourself. Self-talk governs your emotional state, which in turn affects your mental and physical well-being. The following exercise shows you how to shift the balance of power in your self-talk from the negative to the positive.

1. First, determine the number of negative statements you make to yourself during a typical day. Place two jars in your workspace: one filled with coins, the other empty. Every time you have a negative thought, transfer a coin into the empty jar. At the end of the day, count the coins. Are there more coins in the negative thought jar than in the other one?

2. The next day, list twenty-eight negative things that you think about yourself. For example, "I'm no good with computers." Take twenty-eight index cards (one for each day of the next four weeks) and on each card write a positive version of your negative statement or a positive response to it. For example, "I can take a computing course if I want to."

3. At the start of each day, take one card and put it where you will see it often. Whenever you see your card, read it to yourself five times.

4. At the end of the four-week period, repeat step 1. This time, there should be fewer coins in your negative thought jar.

KEEPING AN OPTIMISM JOURNAL

Keeping a journal is an excellent way for you to monitor your progress as you read this book, answer the questionnaires, and do the exercises. By getting into the habit of making regular entries, you will keep track of your feelings, increase your self-awareness, and work toward building a more positive self-image.

You should use your journal above all to record your reactions to key events. As in the example below, analyze how these events made you feel by asking yourself questions, such as "what happened?"; "what did I tell myself about what happened?"; "which aspects of my self-talk were positive?"; "which aspects were negative?"; "how would an optimist explain the situation?"

You can also use these questions to reexamine something that happened longer ago, or you can tailor them to an upcoming event that is worrying you, such as a test, a first date, or trying out for the school play.

Your journal can have all kinds of uses. For example, you can use it to list the things for which you should be grateful, to face your fears, or to track your level of happiness over time (see the "happiness score" below). Taking the time to keep a journal is an important investment in your personal growth. By exploring your reaction to the major and minor events in your life, you can reach a better understanding of how you think—a first step toward increasing your optimism.

DATE

KEY EVENT OF THE DAY	
WHAT DID I TELL MYSELF?	
POSITIVE SELF-TALK	NEGATIVE SELF-TALK
OPTIMISTIC INTERPRETATION	

(1) (2) (3) (4) (5) (6) (7) (8) (9) (10) HAPPINESS SCORE

HAVE I WORRIED ABOUT ANYTHING TODAY?
IF SO, WHY AM I WORRIED?
OPTIMISTIC INTERPRETATION
ACTION PLAN

2

OPTIMISTIC ATTITUDES

It goes with you everywhere you go. It is on display at work and at home. People make judgments about you on the basis of it. It has no color, it has no size, yet its impact on your life is huge. What is it? Your attitude! An optimistic attitude prepares you to anticipate success and to bounce back from setbacks. A positive outlook helps you to view obstacles as opportunities and to stay motivated to achieve what you want in life. With an optimistic attitude, you will make self-fulfilling prophecies work for you rather than against you. If you expect things to turn out well, they are more likely to do so.

This chapter teaches you the thinking skills you will need to optimize your attitude. For example, you will learn to recognize and be grateful for what you have, to stop negative thoughts from spiraling out of control, and to tackle problems with confidence and imagination.

HALF-FULL OR HALF-EMPTY?

Is the glass half-full or half-empty? This is just one of the most common of the many metaphors used to contrast optimism with pessimism. It is also said, tongue in cheek, that an optimist sees daylight at the end of a tunnel, whereas a pessimist sees the headlights of an oncoming train. Optimists believe that every cloud has a silver lining, while pessimists just see the potential for rain. Optimists see the doughnut; pessimists see the hole. Keeping your glass half-full is a matter of what you pay attention to. If you accentuate the positive aspects of a situation, this does not mean that you are denying the negative, it's simply that you are making a conscious decision to seek encouragement rather than discouragement.

One way to focus on the half-full part of the glass is to express gratitude for what you have or what you have experienced. People who show their appreciation report feeling more alert, enthusiastic, energetic, and optimistic, and they experience less stress and depression. There is no doubt that when the going is tough, it is more difficult to be grateful than when things are going well. However, it is during the hard times that we need gratitude the most.

COUNT YOUR BLESSINGS

It is not always easy to recognize the things in our lives for which we should be thankful. And, particularly when we are unhappy, it can be annoying to be told to cheer up and be grateful that we have our home, our family, our health, and so on. However, this is precisely what you should do. This exercise is designed to help you to identify and celebrate your many blessings, even at the times when they seem least apparent to you.

1. Ask yourself "what do I have to be grateful for?" Write down in your optimism journal whatever occurs to you as something you are grateful for. Start with the basics. A roof over your head? Food to eat? Family? Friends? Then list recent positive events, such as goals you have achieved or times when someone has been kind to you.

2. If necessary, take a walk around your home to prompt you. Use all five of your senses. For example, you might be grateful for a favorite song playing at a particular moment, a delicious meal, or the way your bed feels.

3. Look at your list. Think of all the ways in which the items you have written down enrich your life. If you have reason to be grateful to people you know, find a way of showing your appreciation.

4. At the end of the day, review your list of blessings and go to sleep on a positive note.

PREPARING FOR SUCCESS

Not surprisingly, it has been found that successful people have high scores when tested for optimism. But which comes first, the success or the optimism? Research shows that in most cases it is an optimistic attitude that paves the way for success rather than the other way around. Optimists thrive because they believe that they have the skills required to be successful. They reinforce their confidence and motivation both by focusing on their past triumphs and by visualizing the success of future projects. And they have the resilience not to let rejection and failure knock them off course. To prepare yourself for success ask yourself the following questions and write the answers in your journal:

- What do I want to achieve? Describe each goal and your motivation for achieving it in as much detail as possible.
- When do I want this goal to be realized? Draw up a schedule and put it in your agenda.
- What do I need to do to accomplish my vision? Itemize each step and its length, then track your progress.
- Are there any obstacles likely to stand in my way? Anticipate possible pitfalls and ways to deal with them.

- What will it be like when I achieve my goal? Imagine how you will feel. Ask yourself what this project means to you. Use these thoughts to motivate you to carry on when things are not going according to plan.

CREATE ABUNDANCE

Optimists operate with an attitude of abundance. Abundance is being satisfied with what you have, while envisioning what you want. Abundance is believing that there are enough resources available for everyone to get what they want out of life. To help you manifest abundance in your life, try creating an abundance collage. You will need the following materials: a large sheet of poster board, glue, scissors, a marker, and a variety of magazines that you don't mind cutting up.

1. Try to get yourself in a relaxed, creative mood— perhaps by playing some music, by lighting some candles, or by drinking a cup of herbal tea.

2. Start looking through the magazines and tear out any pages that contain things you appreciate in your life or things you hope to have or achieve one day or words that inspire you to live the life you want to live. It may take more than one sitting to gather up all your words and images.

3. Once you've made your selections, paste them onto the poster board. If there are any blank spaces, you can fill them by writing inspiring quotes in them.

4. Put up your collage in a room where you will see it often. Whenever you see your abundance collage, take a moment to enjoy what you already have and to anticipate the good things coming your way.

DEALING WITH SETBACKS

The next time you flick on the light switch, thank Thomas Edison and his ability to overcome setbacks. Edison experimented more than ten thousand times before producing the first incandescent lightbulb in 1879. When asked about his previous failures while trying to discover the secrets of the lightbulb, Thomas Edison is quoted as saying, "I have not failed. I've just found ten thousand ways that won't work." Edison worked with optimism, persistence, and passion to create more than one thousand patented inventions. Some of his other famous inventions include the phonograph, the mimeograph, and the motion-picture camera and projector. Not only do we benefit from his inventions, but we can also learn much from the way that Edison dealt with failure. Adopting his principles, we will see below how setbacks, rather than knocking you off course, can help you get closer to your goal.

Tolerate failure. Failure is an integral part of the process of trying to accomplish something. Be realistic— do not be surprised or disheartened to find obstacles in your way, but believe that you have what it takes to overcome them.

Believe you will succeed the next time. Edison always considered success to be just around the corner. Adopting this attitude will ensure that you channel all your energies into every attempt, increasing your chances of success.

Don't take it personally. Edison did not consider himself to be a poor inventor just because his experiments didn't always work. Likewise, successful salespeople do not blame themselves every time they experience a rejection. If they did, their morale would become so damaged that they would not be able to carry on doing their job. When things go wrong, do not waste time and effort berating yourself. Save your energy for your next attempt.

Keep on keeping on. Thomas Edison did not live on inspiration alone, as he underlined in his now famous quote, "Genius is 1 percent inspiration, 99 percent perspiration." Persistence is one of the keys to achieving your goals. So, if at first you don't succeed . . .

Learn the lessons. Edison considered his failures to be crucial to his success because each of them gave him an opportunity to learn something new. Analyze your setbacks, figure out the lessons from them, and use your newfound insight to focus your next attempt. Look for success within failure. Sometimes when we fail to achieve our target, we may accidentally succeed in accomplishing something else. Think of all the times you have inadvertently strayed from a recipe and invented a delicious dish all your own.

Many of life's failures are people who did not realize how close they were to success when they gave up.

Thomas Edison
(1847–1931)

Similarly, the invention of the Post-it® note in the 1970s was a happy accident—an ingenious application for a failed attempt to develop a strong adhesive. And you will not be surprised to learn that Edison painstakingly documented all his experiments and regularly reviewed his old ideas to spark off new projects. Don't be haunted by your setbacks: be inspired by them. Like Edison, keep a record in your journal of all your attempts to achieve a goal. For each attempt, ask yourself the following questions to help you analyze what happened:

- What was I trying to achieve?
- Why didn't it work?
- Can I identify any successful aspects of the experience?
- What lessons have I learned as a result of this?
- What will I do differently next time?

STOP YOUR THOUGHTS

It is important to set out toward all our goals expecting to succeed. However, sometimes our efforts are hampered by negative thoughts that circle around and around in our minds. Thought stopping is a technique you can use to help you disrupt and discontinue these negative thought processes.

1. Find a quiet, comfortable place to sit. Close your eyes and breathe slowly, deeply, and evenly. Release the tension in your body by contracting and releasing each of your muscles in turn.

2. When you feel relaxed, bring the negative thought that is troubling you into your awareness. Consciously repeat the thought in your mind and after each repetition, say out loud "stop" or "no."

3. Having stopped the negative thought, try to replace it in your mind with a positive statement. For example, if your unwanted thought is "I am too shy for people to like me," you might change that into "I am confident and people like me."

4. With practice, thought stopping will become second nature to you, so that you can even use a condensed

version of the technique in pressure situations, such as class presentations. In settings where talking out loud to yourself would be inappropriate, try imagining a red stop sign instead. Whatever the circumstances, say no to any negative thoughts.

DECIDING WHEN TO BE REALISTIC

Living in the real world, as opposed to an idealized one, is generally felt to be a good thing. However, this may not always be the case. In this section, we will look at the pros and cons of realism, to help you decide when it is better to face facts and when it is better to put them to one side and focus on the hoped-for outcome.

Numerous studies have found that optimists have an unrealistically positive view of themselves and an exaggerated perception of the amount of control they have over events and that their high hopes for the future are often unfounded. They believe that they are more likely than other people to experience positive events and less likely to experience negative events. Although distorted, these "positive illusions" help make optimists happier, healthier, more willing to take on challenges, and better able to deal with setbacks.

Sometimes not facing reality in the short term may act as a valuable defense mechanism. For example, people who are diagnosed with a life-threatening disease often refuse to accept the diagnosis at first. This gives them the time to process the information subconsciously, to gather themselves, and to approach the situation at their own speed. Temporary denial can help us to function in stressful situations by reducing paralyzing anxiety.

In contrast, too much realism can lead to fatalism, helplessness, and depression. Depressive realism is the tendency of depressed people to see things as they really are. It is a "wiser but sadder" approach—people who are depressed may make more accurate judgments, but their unfiltered outlook is one of the things that makes them unhappy. Of course, there are times when an unrealistically optimistic attitude can be dangerous. Unbridled optimism is unsuitable in situations in which you risk paying a very high emotional or physical price if you fail. For example, if your parents were so positive that they were going to win the lottery that they sold your house and borrowed large amounts of money to pay for lottery tickets, then the cost of failing to win would be high indeed.

It may seem strange, but at times such as these, when we have to assess the risks involved in different courses of action, we may benefit from strategic, controlled use of pessimistic thinking. In her book *The Positive Power of Negative Thinking* (2001), psychologist Julie Norem labels this positive use of pessimistic thinking as "defensive pessimism." Norem stresses that defensive pessimists, because they choose to think in this way, are completely different from instinctive pessimists, who dwell on unhappy events and believe that nothing will ever go well for them. Defensive pessimism can be particularly useful when you are feeling anxious in the face of a challenge. At such a time, your expectations of success may be low, but you can increase your confidence by preempting what might go wrong and preparing a back-up plan for the worst-case scenario. This strategy helps you to manage your anxiety and perform your best.

Defensive pessimism doesn't work for everybody. Nonanxious people tend to use what Norem terms "strategic optimism." They protect themselves from anxiety by expecting the best and refusing to let a sense of reality remind them what might go wrong—an approach that might feel uncomfortable for someone who tends toward anxiety and might cause his or her performance to suffer.

The beauty of defensive pessimism is that you can decide when to use it. When facing a challenge, weigh what you risk losing against what you stand to gain. Use defensive pessimism when the stakes are high and strategic optimism when the risk is something you can live with. We have seen that pessimists often make more accurate assessments than optimists. However, when things are tough, it is easy to find yourself viewing the world in an unrealistically negative light. Try this simple exercise to get you back in touch with what you know to be true for you. It will help you to build your inner strength and reassure you so that you can stay the course.

WHAT I KNOW TO BE TRUE

1. Write "What I know to be true" at the top of a page in your journal. Create a list of the good things that you know to be true in your life. For example: "I know that Sue loves me" or "I know that I am friendly."

2. Whenever the world seems bleak, revisit your list and update it if appropriate. Remind yourself of all the good things you know to be true.

   I know . . .
   • One person who loves me
   • Something I am good at
   • Something that makes me laugh
   • One way that I take care of myself
   • One thing I enjoy doing
   • My favorite pastime
   • One thing I like about where I live

- A kindness someone showed me
- One way that I behave responsibly

TAKING ACTION

One of the most common sources of unhappiness is letting unsatisfactory situations continue unnecessarily. It's one thing to realize that you need to pull yourself out of a predicament. But it's quite another thing to know where to start—and to actually make that start. Wanting to change is important, but there is no substitute for action. One of the reasons we can get stuck and not take action is that we overanalyze our thoughts about the way we are thinking —talk about analysis paralysis! The first question to ask yourself is "Is the change I want to make worth my effort?" If the answer is yes, read on.

Taking action without thoughtful preparation is like setting sail without a compass or a map. Imagine you are miserable in a class that you've been struggling through for a long time, but you see no way of making a breakthrough. You are stuck. In this situation, you need to come to grips with precisely what it is that is troubling you. Perhaps it's to do with the material, lack of stimulation, a pressure to succeed in everything, or the feeling that you are not making a valuable contribution or have nowhere to go next with this subject. Or perhaps you just need a change. But feeling restless and deciding that you'll seize the next opportunity that comes along is not a recipe for turning your life around. Better to look out for—or make for yourself—an opportunity that addresses your particular dissatisfactions.

A written analysis is always a good place to start—clearly stating what you want to change helps you to define your goals and avoid distractions. The advantage of detailed self-analysis is that it gives you a way to turn a negative view of your situation—"I don't want to do my homework anymore"—into a positive view, a set of goals that in turn you can convert into a program of action, step by step, creating a natural rhythm of change.

Once you know what you are aiming for, taking steps to achieve it will automatically make you feel more positive. Taking action is energizing and empowering and will help you feel better about the future. Even looking up information on the internet should be enough to refocus your mind on a realistic prospect of change. You know where you want to go; and you have started taking measures to get there. Once you have set wheels in motion, you'll find that they take you along with them with a new momentum. Things start to happen, prompting a response from you. With your master plan in mind, you react in ways that serve you. At last, you are following your sense of purpose in a spirit of optimism. Setbacks may occur, but the energy of change is too strong for them to throw you off-course for long. Through flexible thinking and creative problem solving, you continue to make progress. Whenever you reach a key stage along the way, take the time to enjoy your accomplishment. Register how good it feels and use this memory to spur you on to further achievements. Here are some tips for sharpening your action skills:

Take responsibility for creating the change that you want. Other people may be able to help you, but the driving force behind the process must come from within you.

Get out of your comfort zone. You need to challenge the way you have always done things.

Take control of your time. Dedicate a specific amount of time to creating a plan and putting it into action.

Surround yourself with positive people, to encourage you along the way. Negative people can drain your energy by discouraging you when you try to accomplish something new.

There is no excuse for excuses. Stop wasting your energy coming up with reasons why you can't and channel your energy into finding ways in which you can.

Don't be governed by your moods. If you wait until you feel like doing it, you may never do it, so choose to be disciplined instead of waiting for your mood to change.

Let go of perfectionism. If you refuse to accept anything less than perfection, then the danger of failure will make it impossible to motivate yourself to embark on a project. Lower your standards in order to get started.

Now—right now—is the time to take action. To start the process, answer these questions in your journal:

- What do I want to change?
- What attitudes are holding me back?
- What will it cost me to try to make this change?

- What will it cost me if I don't try?
- In what ways will my life be improved if I make the change?
- What will I need to do to make this change happen? (If you don't know yet, write down the names of people who can advise you on this.)
- What is one thing that I can do today to move forward?

PROBLEM SOLVING

Your ability to deal with a problem depends greatly on how you view it. If you see it as an obstacle towering over you, you will feel overwhelmed, discouraged, and incompetent, making you more likely to give up. However, if you remind yourself that the problem is temporary and changeable and that it presents you with an opportunity to improve yourself, you will tackle it expecting to succeed, making it more likely that you will.

Although you need to understand a difficulty in order to overcome it, you should try to look beyond the problem and focus instead on the solution. Ask yourself solution-focused questions. For example, when is the problem not there or when do you experience it less? This question helps you to look for exceptions to the problem, rather than thinking that it is everywhere and that it affects everything. Sometimes the solutions are in the exceptions. What is it that makes the problem go away at times? What can you do to make that the case all the time?

A simple example: perhaps you have trouble contributing to class discussions. After a while, you realize that it's only morning classes that are a problem, and that it's only started happening since you gave up eating breakfast. When searching for a solution to a problem, it is important to think creatively and flexibly, to come up with a variety of ideas and to look at the situation from different perspectives. If you are too rigid in your approach, you risk dismissing valuable ideas before giving them adequate consideration.

USE YOUR RIGHT BRAIN

Your brain is divided into the left and right hemispheres. The left brain is primarily responsible for language functions and analytical thinking and processes information in a linear fashion. The right brain excels in spatial and visual awareness, recognizing patterns, and processing information globally. The following exercise is based on the concept of "mind mapping®," devised by the mind-power author and lecturer Tony Buzan.

This is a right-brain method that can be used to tackle problems creatively. You will need a large piece of paper and some colored markers.

1. In the center of the sheet, sketch a picture, cut out an image from a magazine, or use a word to denote your problem and draw a circle around it.

2. Write down or draw the main aspects of the problem around the central circle, linking them to the circle with lines and using a different color for each. So if your problem was needing to lose weight, the key areas might be "diet," "exercise," "schedule," "motivation." Sticking to your color code, draw subbranches out from each area to show ways of addressing each of these issues, potential pitfalls, ways around the pitfalls. Be instinctive—don't edit.

3. You have formulated your plan with your right brain. Now evaluate it with the left brain, eliminating certain ideas and pursuing others.

Brainstorming is another great way to generate ideas. Quickly make a list of potential solutions. All ideas are acceptable—do not try to evaluate them at this stage. Encourage yourself to think fast by placing a time limit on your brainstorming. Next, write each of the ideas on a Post-it® note. Stick the notes on the wall around you and evaluate your ideas objectively. Taking each in turn, ask yourself questions such as "What can go right with this idea?" and "What can go wrong?" Play out as many outcomes as you can, eliminating unpromising ideas as you go by peeling the relevant notes off the wall and leaving the ideas that have merit. When you have evaluated everything in front of you, expand the surviving ideas.

Consider the opportunities that your ideas present and write out an action plan for each one. Itemize all the stages involved, draw up a realistic schedule, and list the resources you will need to make your ideas happen. Be aware of any assumptions or judgments that you make during the process and challenge them. Make an effort to stamp out any negative patterns of thinking. Finally, consider what it will be like for you when the problem no longer exists (or is greatly reduced). Imagining a future without the problem will motivate you to make the necessary changes.

FLEX YOUR THINKING WITH FAMOUS PEOPLE

It can be difficult to assess problems from viewpoints other than your own, but different perspectives can unlock imaginative solutions. Use this exercise to develop your mental flexibility.

1. Clearly define your challenge. For example, "I want to win a race for the track team, but I haven't been running lately."

2. Choose four or five famous people you look to as role models because of a specific philosophy that they are known for or a skill that they have. Imagine what advice they would give you. For example, the golfer Tiger Woods might say, "Just focus your energy on one thing at a time, improve your skills and continue to think that you are the world's best." Mother Theresa might tell you, "Look for an opportunity to volunteer in the type of job that you are seeking so you can gain some experience. By helping others, you help yourself."

3. Ask yourself what would happen if you took the imaginary advice offered by your role models. "What would happen if I listened to Tiger Woods and took things one step at a time? What would happen if I improved my skills in the meantime? What if I told myself I was the world's best?"

4. Use your "what would happen if" thoughts to explore different perspectives whenever you are feeling discouraged, lazy, or stressed.

SELF-FULFILLING PROPHECIES

Betty is nervous about meeting her boyfriend's parents for the first time. "They won't like me," she frets. "All they're interested in is the opera. As usual, I won't fit in. They'll probably just ignore me. I'll stay quiet and not let on that I don't know anything about opera." Sure enough, the evening turns into a disaster. Betty remains silent and aloof while Allan's parents speak enthusiastically about the latest opera production. To begin, they make polite attempts to include her, but when she fails to reciprocate they stop trying, and she is ignored. Betty's own actions ensure that her prophecy comes true.

This imaginary episode illustrates just how much influence we have over upcoming events—for better or, in this case, for worse. Our expectations first govern our intentions, which regulate our behavior, which affects the behavior of the other people involved. Betty's expectation that her boyfriend's parents would not like her led to her intention not to draw attention to herself, which led to her silent behavior, which, in turn, led to their ignoring her. Seeing your prophecy come true reinforces the beliefs behind it, making a similar scenario even more likely to occur in the future. The prediction that is most likely to influence whether we succeed or fail is the one that we make about our ability to succeed—a measure known as self-efficacy. As the psychologist Albert Bandura stated, self-efficacy "is not the skills one has but rather one's judgment of what one can do with those skills." If you can increase your level of self-efficacy, your self-fulfilling prophecies will invariably be positive—you will tackle situations in the expectation of success and you will expect other people to view you in a positive light, which will inspire them to do so. For example, if Betty had said to herself, "OK, I may not know much about opera, but I can show Allan's parents that I am interested in what they have to say, and there are plenty of other things I can talk to them about," then it is more than likely that her evening would have turned out much better.

You can learn to make more positive predictions about your competence (your self-efficacy) and how others will treat you, which will lead to more of your endeavors going well. One way to increase your self-efficacy is to draw inspiration from the successes of your friends. Rather than using their achievements as a way to discourage yourself, examine the factors that enabled them to succeed. Think about all the hard work they had to invest, and remind yourself that if they can do it, there's no reason why you can't achieve something similar.

Another method is to seek encouraging feedback from someone whose opinion you value. Go to that valued person and describe to them the problem that you are struggling with—they will generally be able to give you a more objective and more positive assessment of your ability to meet the challenge than you can muster. Even if you are not able to call on the assistance of a real person, the exercise opposite shows how you can conduct this kind of conversation with yourself.

Use empathy to predict other people's reactions to you in a more positive way. Instead of jumping to the conclusion that they will view you negatively, try to anticipate your dealings with them through their eyes. How would you judge you in their position? (This will help you realize that others will almost certainly judge you more favorably than you judge yourself.) Do you have any ill feeling toward them? Probably not. In which case, why do you insist on assuming that they will think badly of you? The self-fulfilling prophecy is an immensely powerful tool. Make sure you use it to build yourself up, not to knock yourself down. Listen to Henry Ford's words: "If you think you can do a thing or think you can't do a thing, you're right."

WHAT DO YOU EXPECT?

If your expectations are low when undertaking something new, try the "empty chair" technique, which comes from Gestalt therapy, a version of psychotherapy that focuses on people recognizing and changing the assumptions that hinder them. This role-playing exercise gives you the chance to express your expectations, examine them, and come up with a more constructive prediction.

1. In a room by yourself, sit in a chair, facing another, empty, chair. Picture a virtual version of yourself

sitting in the empty chair.

2. Speaking out loud to your virtual self, state your negative expectations about the upcoming event, but add a positive ending. If, say, you are worried about starting at a new school or college, you might tell yourself: "I expect all the other students to be smarter than you and that they will not like you, but you can change that expectation."

3. Now, argue for your right to expect to be successful: "When you started high school, you felt the same way you are feeling now, but you did really well and made lots of great friends—the same will happen when you go to off to college."

4. When stating your new expectations, feel your newfound confidence and optimism. Draw yourself up in your chair. By changing your expectations, you are helping the self-fulfilling prophecy to work in your favor.

BUILDING CONFIDENCE

As we have seen, optimists possess many valuable qualities, such as self-awareness, resilience, and happiness. However, no attribute is more precious to the optimist than his or her self-confidence. By trusting in your ability to do what needs to be done, you enter into all your undertakings in the expectation of success. Expecting to succeed is a powerful motivator and helps you to persist even in the face of difficulties. And, of course, positive expectations tend to lead to positive results.

It is not true, as some assert, that self-confident people are conceited. Self-confident people have their doubts and negative thoughts about themselves and their abilities. It's just that they have the self-awareness to recognize these thoughts and replace them with positive alternatives. Do not confuse bragging with confidence; genuinely confident people do not need to bring attention to themselves or their accomplishments or denigrate other people in order to feel happy about themselves.

Whereas confident people expect success, those who lack confidence often do so because they fear failure. This fear creates a vicious circle of self-doubt. If you never attempt anything, for fear of failing, you will lack the memory store of past achievements that optimists can draw upon to build their confidence. When fear controls you instead of you controlling your fear, it is time to devise a plan of action. This may seem daunting at first, but by breaking the process down into the following stages, you will be able to shift from a vicious circle of fear to a virtuous circle of confidence.

Face your fears. In your optimism journal, make a list of all the aspects of a particular challenge that frighten you and stop you from attempting it. For example, if you lack the confidence to speak in public, you might write down such things as "I might forget what to say next in my speech;" "People might laugh at me;" "They might think I am stupid." Examine each of your concerns in turn. Are they really possible? Imagine if they did happen—would it really be so bad? Put your fears in their place by writing down an optimistic response to each of your statements. For example, "I might forget what to say next in my speech— but that's not the end of the world."

Take things one step at a time. Confidence is best developed through a series of small successes that build on one another. To aim too high without going through the intermediate steps is to risk returning to a cycle of failure and self-doubt. Again taking public speaking as an example, the first step might be to join your school's debate and speech club, which teaches people how to speak with confidence. Gain self-assurance in this way, before moving on to speaking in classroom discussions on a regular basis, and only then consider tackling a larger audience.

Be prepared. Do not risk your growing confidence by taking on a challenge without adequate planning and practice. Feeling that you are in a position to do your best will increase your self-confidence and can help you to overcome last-minute jitters. Keep up the positive self-talk —for example, by repeating to yourself over and over "I can do this."

Act confident. Remember that your body language influences the way you feel and the way other people perceive you. Look people in the eyes when you speak to them, hold your head up, speak in a steady voice, and smile.

Beware of "all or nothing" thinking. This is a trap that perfectionists set for themselves. Unless the outcome is perfect, the perfectionist thinks that he or she has failed completely. It is far more constructive to focus on what went well.

Bask in your achievements. Once you have mastered your challenge, take time to accept praise from yourself and others. Reward yourself for having the courage to face your fear and come out the other side. Create a "My Successes" page in your journal where you record the details of your achievements.

VISUALIZE CONFIDENCE

Visualization is a type of meditation that involves using your imagination to change how you feel. This exercise is designed to help you increase your confidence by seeing yourself achieve a goal.

1. Picture a scenario that requires you to act with confidence—for example, trying out for the school play. Use all your senses to set the scene—in this case, you might imagine the smell of the coffee from the

director's cup or the sound of the photocopier just outside the door.

2. Write down the way you want the scenario to develop, going into as much detail as possible. For example, who will be there?; how do you want to feel?; what do you want to say?; how do you want the play's director to respond to you?

3. Summarize your description point by point and read it over until you remember the steps.

4. Now that you have committed your visualization to memory, it is time to play it out. Relax, and breathe slowly, evenly, and deeply. With your eyes closed, imagine every detail of the scene, playing it in your mind like a movie. Picture yourself acting confidently in all phases of the scenario and imagine how it feels to be confident.

5. Practice your visualization whenever you need to build your confidence.

REFRAMING YOUR THOUGHTS

Reframing is a strategy that optimists use to find the positive meaning in seemingly negative situations. By actively choosing to view a difficult problem in a positive light, you automatically gain some control over it, which helps to reduce your feelings of distress and anxiety and promotes your well-being and your motivation to overcome the problem no matter what.

If you want a simple demonstration of the power of reframing, visit an art shop. Take a picture and hold a variety of frames to it. See how different the picture looks with each frame. Different types of frames highlight different aspects of the picture and can even influence the overall mood evoked by the image. It is only by changing the frame that you come to appreciate the effect of the original frame. Similarly, it is only by attempting to alter your frame of reference that you can see how a negative attitude to a difficult situation hinders your ability to deal with it.

Reframing involves two main stages. The first step is to understand your original frame by asking yourself, "What do I feel about this situation? And what do these feelings make me want to do about the situation?" The next step is to create a new frame of reference by looking at your circumstances in a positive manner. Using the everyday example of narrowly missing a bus, your first thought might be "What an idiot I am! If I had walked a little faster, I would have caught that bus. Now I'm going to have to wait around for an hour, and I'll get to school late." Your reframe might be "Now I can read that history chapter a little slower and understand it better."

The above example works by identifying the unexpected benefit—the blessing in disguise—in adverse circumstances and exploiting it. This is a fundamental reframing technique.

However, other situations may require different reframing techniques. In some cases, it may be helpful to break down the problem by understanding what caused it in the first place: "Our roof is leaking simply because a tile was damaged in the storm. Mom will replace the tile and then our roof will not leak anymore." Another reframing method is to repackage a problem as a challenge. For example, you could reframe a particularly stressful time at school by telling yourself: "Studying's really interesting at the moment. There are lots of problems to fix—it will give me a chance to show what I can do."

Your new frame doesn't always have to be custom built. Start collecting ready-made attitude statements that you can use to reframe your reaction to temporary difficulties. Examples include: "It could be worse;" "Everything happens for a reason;" and "This will not matter next week." If you lost your wallet, you could tell yourself: "It's not that bad. It's only money. Some people have much bigger problems to deal with." Even if these thoughts come to you automatically, they still have meaning.

We have seen how reframing your thoughts enables you to cope with relatively minor setbacks. However, it can also help you to come to terms with traumatic events, such as a family member being diagnosed with a serious illness or suffering a loss in your family. At these times, our belief in life's fairness can be shaken. Salvaging positive meaning and seeing your experience as part of a bigger picture can help to reduce the psychological harm of the trauma.

People often search for the meaning of tragic events within their religious or spiritual beliefs. Your faith, coupled with the support of a religious community, can be a source of reassurance in difficult times. For this reason, religious faith and spirituality are associated with optimism and resilience.

Changing the frame will not magically make the picture seem rosy, but it may help you to accept, and to learn from, your loss.

LOOK FOR THE SILVER LINING

Finding something positive in an adverse situation is not always easy. This exercise is designed to guide you in your search by helping you to analyze your circumstances in a structured way.

1. Take a piece of paper or a page in your journal and draw three columns. In the first column, define the situation that you are facing, for example "starting at a new school."

2. In the middle column, describe your initial interpretation of the situation. Are you worried, upset, angry? What is making you feel that way? Using the example in step 1: "I feel anxious—no one will know me."

3. In the third column, list ways to reinterpret your circumstances positively. For example: "I'm not anxious, I'm excited;" "I can use my anxiety to motivate me to do well;" or "I don't know anyone, so this will be a great chance to meet lots of interesting new people." To prompt you, ask yourself some of the following questions: What good can come from this situation? What lessons can I apply to the future? What strengths do I have as a result? What else could this experience mean?

4. If you are struggling, ask a trusted friend to help you generate some ideas. However, with practice, you will find that positive reinterpretation becomes a positive habit.

OPTIMISM AND YOUR PHYSICAL HEALTH

Your head and your body are linked by more than just your neck. There is compelling evidence to show that your attitude exerts a powerful influence over your physical health. Optimistic people, who experience a variety of positive emotions, such as happiness and self-belief, tend to have stronger immune systems, to recover more quickly from surgery, and to live longer than more pessimistic people. The mind–body connection also works in the opposite direction: taking good care of your body, by eating well and exercising regularly, has a positive impact on your mood. In this chapter, we will look at ways to take control of your health: how to monitor your physical well-being, how to view illness and pain as challenges to overcome rather than ordeals to endure, and how to incorporate the principles of healthy living into your daily routine.

THE MIND-BODY CONNECTION

Take a few seconds to close your eyes and imagine that you are chewing on a slice of lemon. Did your mouth water? If so, this is just one example of how the mind can affect the body. Likewise, the body influences the mind, which explains why exercise often makes us feel happy. By understanding and exploiting the mind–body connection, we can exert a significant and beneficial influence on our physical and mental well-being.

There are many scientific sources of evidence for the powerful interaction between the psychological and the physical. For example, psychoneuroimmunology looks at how emotions and behaviors, particularly those associated with stress, directly impact the immune system. Although stress is initially a psychological experience, it also provokes a physical response in the form of increased production of adrenaline (epinephrine), which makes muscles tense, and breathing shallow and rapid. Adrenaline also destroys white blood cells, which are crucial to a healthy immune system. Therefore, if you suffer from chronic stress, your adrenaline level will be at a constant high and you will be more likely to fall ill.

The greatest force in the human body is the natural drive of the body to heal itself, but that force is not independent of the belief system . . . everything begins with belief.

Norman Cousins
(1915–1990)

On the other hand, if you lower your stress levels—for example, by changing your attitude to difficult situations, stretching your muscles, and regulating your breathing—you will support your immune system and help protect yourself from illness.

The placebo effect is another important aspect of the mind–body connection. Numerous studies have shown that if a patient believes that taking a particular medicine will alleviate his or her symptoms, then the patient's condition will indeed improve, even if the drug is a placebo—that is to say, a fake dose. This has led researchers to discover that our beliefs about a treatment have an effect on our neurochemistry, which in turn affects our bodies.

Other research has suggested that faith in its widest sense can help people to stay healthy. Spirituality has been shown, among other things, to ward off depression, accelerate recovery from illness, and help people to adjust to disability. One study indicated that people who attend religious services at least once a week have stronger immune systems than people who do not actively practice a religion. Dr. Herbert Benson, author of *Timeless Healing: The Power and Biology of Belief* (1996), claims that 60 percent of an average individual's visits to the doctor are provoked by stress-related illnesses, but that among people who describe themselves as spiritual this figure goes down to between 35 and 50 percent.

This link between spirituality and health has given rise to another strand of research focusing on how physicians can tap into their patients' faith to help them recover from illness. A recent study led by J. Lebron McBride, an expert in behavioral medicine, found that when doctors took account of their patients' spiritual beliefs in their treatment (for example, by suggesting that they seek support from their spiritual community), these patients got better more quickly than others with similar conditions.

However, you do not have to subscribe to any belief system in order to reap the health benefits of a positive attitude. A 2000 study by the Mayo Clinic found that optimists tend to live longer than expected, whereas pessimists are more likely to die prematurely. To develop an optimistic approach to your health, you need to foster a sense of personal control. Rather than ignoring a health problem and hoping it will go away, take charge by seeking medical care at an early stage. And if you or a family member are diagnosed with an illness, try to view it as a challenge to overcome, rather than as a source of suffering that you are powerless to affect.

There are specific mind–body therapies you can use to take control of your health, including meditation, yoga, and hypnosis. By allowing you to enter a relaxed state of deep concentration and opening your mind to suggestion, hypnosis can help you, among other things, to overcome anxiety and depression, manage pain, and conquer addictions.

OPTIMISM AND YOGA

Yoga is a holistic way to become healthier, physically and mentally. Studies show that yoga postures and breathing techniques decrease anxiety, depression, and chronic pain and increase optimism, self-confidence, concentration, and calmness. Take a yoga class or rent a yoga video and try out this wonderful method of moving meditation.

Controlling the breath is fundamental to the practice of yoga and requires concentration. While you are applying your mind to your breathing, you can't think of anything else—it gives you a mental break from the rest of your life, leaving you calmer and more able to think positively.

Pranayama: **The Yoga Breath**

If you are looking for a fast and sure method to change your mood, try the following yoga breath. The calming effect of pranayama works as a quick-fix response to a stressful situation or lightens your mood when you are feeling down. You can do this anywhere, anytime. Pranayama can be performed sitting down, standing or lying on your back. Allow your abdomen to expand when inhaling and relax when you exhaling.

- Breathe in through your nostrils, into the lower part of your lungs and expand your abdomen, filling up the middle of the lungs, and finally expand the upper chest.
- Hold your breath for a few seconds.
- Slowly exhale through your nose while drawing in your abdomen.
- Relax, take a few regular breaths, then repeat five to ten times.
- Practice this breath until you can do it in a continuous motion.

MANAGING YOUR HEALTH

Would you describe yourself as healthy? Be careful with your answer, as it plays a greater part than you might think in determining how healthy you actually are. As with so many aspects of the mind–body connection, if you believe that you are healthy, your health will actually benefit.

Health perception has been the subject of a large amount of research. One study found that people who were pessimistic about their health despite having been given a clean bill of health from the doctor tended to die slightly sooner than health optimists whose health was described as poor by their doctors. In another study conducted at Duke University in North Carolina, three thousand heart patients were asked to rate their health as poor, fair, good, or very good. The ones who described their health as poor were approximately three times more likely to die within the following three years than those who chose very good.

So, managing your perception of your health is an integral part of managing your health. Optimists believe that they have within themselves the power to control many aspects of their lives, and their health is no exception. This belief is known as an internal locus of control. Not only does this sense of control influence your attitude toward your health, but it also determines your behavior. For example, optimists will seek early treatment from their doctors, will comply if asked to follow specific treatments, and are likely to eat healthy foods and exercise

DO YOU FEEL IN CONTROL OF YOUR HEALTH?

This questionnaire, adapted with permission from Dr. Ken Wallston, enables you to assess your "health locus of control" (the extent to which you feel in control of your health). Use the following scale to show how far you identify with each of the statements below.

1 = Strongly disagree; 2 = Moderately disagree;
3 = Slightly disagree; 4 = Slightly agree;
5 = Moderately agree; 6 = Strongly agree

⬭ If I get sick, it is my own behavior that determines how soon I recover.

⬭ I am in control of my health.

⬭ When I get sick, I am to blame.

⬭ The main thing that affects my health is what I myself do.

⬭ If I take care of myself, I can avoid illness.

⬭ If I take the right actions, I can stay healthy.

A score of 25 or more indicates a highly internal locus of control; between 13 and 24 is average; and 12 or below suggests a particularly external locus of control.

regularly. They do all this because they believe it will make a difference to their health, which, of course, it does. On the other hand, pessimists are trapped in a state of learned helplessness. They don't see the point of stopping smoking, and they don't exercise because they believe that no action will make any difference to their health. Their locus of control is external.

If the answers you give to the questionnaire in the sidebar suggest that you have an external locus of control in relation to your health, there are simple ways to take control. The following sections in this chapter will explain how, by developing positive exercise, eating, and sleeping habits, you can actively improve your health. You should also take control of monitoring your health. Establish a routine of check-ups and screenings. Preventive screenings, such as measuring blood pressure and cholesterol and testing for common cancers, can alert doctors to problems at an early stage, which makes it easier to treat them and more likely that you will recuperate fully. The exercise on the following page outlines how you can use a health diary to help your doctor to gain a clear understanding of any symptoms you experience.

This hands-on approach may sound like a recipe for hypochondria. However, managing your health does not mean seeking problems that don't exist, it's more about putting in place a framework to promote good health and dealing with problems if they arise. In fact, by making your health care a matter of routine, the business of taking care of yourself takes care of itself.

KEEP A HEALTH DIARY

A health diary is an invaluable tool for managing your health in partnership with the various health care professionals that you encounter over a lifetime. It enables you to keep track of your health history (in case your official medical records go astray) and to record details of symptoms, which will help your doctor to give an accurate diagnosis and recommend suitable treatment.

1. Use a blank journal or a specially designed health diary. Start by retrospectively recording as much of your personal medical history as you can recall, including any immunizations, childhood illnesses, allergies, hospitalizations, operations, screening results, and prescribed medications, as well as genetic conditions present within your family. Keep track of every doctor's appointment by listing the date, doctor's name, the reason for the visit, symptoms if ill, and tests done. Update your history as necessary.

2. If you suffer from a chronic condition, such as rheumatoid arthritis or asthma, describe any symptoms you experience. How often do they arise

and for how long? Describe any pain you feel, noting its location, nature, and intensity. It might also be useful to keep track of what you have eaten. This may help your doctor to identify a link between your diet and your symptoms.

3. As a precaution, tell a family member or friend where you keep your health diary.

STAY HEALTHY, STAY HAPPY

It is easy to overlook the key role that your body plays in influencing your mood. When you feel unhappy, you may find yourself blaming, say, school pressures or uncertainty about the future. You may even convince yourself that you have a naturally melancholic temperament. However, it could just be that you've been cooped up at your desk for too long, you've been eating too much unhealthy food or skipping meals, you're feeling dissatisfied (rightly or wrongly) with your weight, or you've been missing out on sleep. As we will see in the following sections, you can overcome problems in any of these areas—exercise, diet, weight control, and sleep—without dramatically overhauling your life: no therapy, no big change, just a series of small steps toward health, happiness, and a more positive outlook.

PLAN YOUR EXERCISE ROUTINE

Once you have obtained permission from your doctor to start or resume an exercise program, the next step is planning. Planning helps you to deal with the two biggest obstacles to exercising on a regular basis: lack of time and lack of motivation.

1. Decide on the best time of the day to exercise. Pick the time when you are most likely to stick to your routine. You will be more motivated to exercise when your energy levels are high. Are you a morning person or do you function better in the afternoon or evening?

2. Consider how long your exercise sessions will last. They need not all be the same length. If you can spare only fifteen minutes on a Monday but a full hour on a Thursday, take that into account. The key is to keep the routine easy and accessible. Psychologically, you will feel better if you have stuck to your plan, and you will stay motivated.

3. Schedule your exercise time into your agenda or diary. Writing it down will help you to stick to your routine, just as you would with a meeting with the school newspaper or football practice.

4. Practice exercise that you find fun. Run, bike, swim, or go to an aerobics or other class. Doing exercise that you like in your preferred location is important if you are to keep coming back for more.

GET SOME EXERCISE

The number one mood-enhancing tool at your disposal is exercise. On a psychological level, exercise provides you with a distraction from the stressful things in your life—a short break from your worries. It also enables you to aim for clearly defined goals, such as a personal-best time for a regular running route, the achievement of which is a great confidence booster. Perhaps this is why exercise has been shown to increase self-esteem.

Exercise also makes you feel good on a biochemical level by causing your body to release endorphins, which induce a sense of euphoria known as the runner's high. Not only do endorphins make you feel happy, but they also enhance the immune system, relieve pain, and reduce stress.

You do not have to be an elite athlete, training yourself to the limit for hours each day, to enjoy the psychological benefits of exercise. Research has found that it is frequency of exercise, rather than length or intensity, that wards off depression. You should aim to exercise for thirty minutes five times each week. Use your agenda to plan a routine. Remember that an exercise session doesn't have to involve traveling to a gym—it could be as simple as taking a half-hour walk during your lunch break or spending time gardening in the evening or on the weekend. One word of caution: if you are not exercising regularly at this point, check with your doctor before you start.

EAT SMART

It is no secret that a healthy, balanced diet provides your body with the range of nutrients it requires to function effectively, including to maintain your energy levels, to strengthen your muscles and bones, and to support your immune system. However, the food you eat also influences the way your brain works—your ability to concentrate and, importantly, the endurance of your mood. While eating a generally healthy diet will help you to feel happy, there are certain specific aspects of nutrition that you can focus on to regulate your mood.

If you find that your mood, your energy, and concentration levels fluctuate during an average day, you may need to take steps to maintain a steady blood-sugar level. It is when your blood-sugar level drops that you are particularly likely to become irritable, unhappy, or confused. To stop this from happening, make sure that you do not go too long without eating. Above all, you should never skip breakfast. If you do not eat breakfast, you may find yourself going up to eighteen hours without food, which plays havoc with your blood-sugar level. If you can, it is a good idea to eat five or six small meals each day—this will help to even out your energy production and your mood. Try to cut down your consumption of caffeine, sugar, and highly processed foods, which all lead to a sudden release of sugar into your bloodstream followed by a similarly sudden slump. Instead, maximize your intake of complex carbohydrates, such as those to be found in whole grains, nuts, and seeds, which release sugar more slowly.

Your mood also relies upon your liver and bowels being able to detoxify your system. As well as damaging your physical health, the retention of toxins in your body impedes the flow of serotonin, one of the "feel-good" neurotransmitters in your brain, leaving you feeling gloomy and lacking in motivation. To help your gut to eliminate toxins, eat fewer processed and fast foods—the fat and sugar that they often contain interferes with the digestive process. At the same time, make sure that you eat plenty of fresh fruit and vegetables, as well as whole grains and beans. These foods are high in fiber, which keeps your gut moving, and antioxidants, which aid detoxification.

However, forcing yourself to follow too strict a dietary regime may be counter-productive. The mood-boosting benefits outlined above may be outweighed by a demoralizing sense of privation. Therefore, you should allow yourself occasional sugary or fatty treats—whatever you happen to miss. Indeed, certain high-fat, high-carbohydrate foods, such as ice cream and chocolate, have been found to raise serotonin levels, which is perhaps why they are sometimes known as comfort foods. For women, a particularly good time to seek such comfort is shortly before the start of their period: studies have shown that women's serotonin levels tend to dip at this point in their menstrual cycle.

MANAGE YOUR WEIGHT

Many people are unhappy about their weight, and there is even evidence that being overweight can lead to depression. However, many of the people whose weight makes them unhappy are at a healthy weight. If you are dissatisfied with your weight, try calculating your body mass index, or BMI. You may well find that your perception is distorted. If so, try to stop the negative self-talk that is causing your dissatisfaction.

If, however, your BMI calculation confirms your impression that you are overweight, taking positive steps to manage your weight will make you feel happier. Be wary of radical, "quick-fix" diet plans. The best, most sustainable strategy for losing weight is also the simplest: eat a balanced, healthy diet and follow a program of regular, appropriate exercise. As well as helping you to lose weight, such an approach will give you the sense of control over your life that is central to being an optimist.

SLEEP WELL

Although experts disagree on precisely how sleep supports mental and physical health, all agree that getting enough of it is essential. Some experts believe that when we are asleep, our tissue-repair systems go into overdrive, which would make good-quality sleep an important aspect of the healing process. Others have shown that sleep deprivation weakens the immune system, leaving you susceptible to infections, such as colds and flu. Sleep has a direct impact on your mind and emotions. People who sleep well feel alert and energetic and experience positive emotions, including calmness and satisfaction with life. In contrast, lack of sleep is associated with lethargy, poor concentration, and forgetfulness and negative moods such as apathy, anger, anxiety, and sadness.

CALCULATING YOUR BODY MASS INDEX

Body mass index (BMI) is a commonly accepted measure that health professionals use to assess the suitability of an adult person's weight in relation to his or her height. It is easy to calculate and interpret your own BMI using one of the following two formulas (depending on whether you prefer to use imperial or metric measurements):

BMI = [weight in pounds] ÷ [height in inches] ÷ [height in inches] x 703
or BMI = [weight in kg] ÷ [height in cm] ÷ [height in cm] x 10,000

Using as an example, a man who is six feet tall and weighs 175 pounds, the BMI calculation would be: 175 ÷ 72 ÷ 72 x 703 = 23.7. Adults are generally considered underweight if their BMI is less than 18.5, normal weight if their BMI falls between 18.5 and 24.9, overweight if their BMI is between 25 and 29.9 and obese if it is 30 or more.

Most of us have trouble sleeping at one time or another. And the more we worry about not getting to sleep, the harder it becomes to do so. However, there are many practical ways to break this cycle of anxiety. It is important to follow a prebedtime routine in order to condition your mind and body to expect sleep. Reduce the stimuli you receive in the hour or so before you go to bed by turning down the lighting and switching off the TV. Have a light, protein-rich snack or drink, such as a glass of milk. Protein stimulates the production of serotonin, which, among its many other benefits, helps us to get to sleep. On the other hand, you should avoid caffeine. If, when you lie in bed trying to fall asleep, your mind is preoccupied with a problem, don't stay there tossing, turning, and fretting: get out of bed, write down something constructive you can do tomorrow to address the problem, do some gentle stretching exercises, and go back to bed.

FACING SERIOUS ILLNESS

Coping with serious or even life-threatening illness in your family, such as cancer or heart disease, is a challenge like no other. As you struggle to understand what your family member's diagnosis means to you, you can expect to fall prey to a wide range of negative emotions, such as anxiety, fear, helplessness, anger, and sadness.

Although it is hard to compare scientifically the success of optimists and pessimists in overcoming serious illness, there is plenty of anecdotal evidence to suggest the value of a positive attitude in these circumstances. One of the most notable stories is that of Christopher Reeve, the late actor, who became a quadriplegic after sustaining a spinal cord injury in a horseback riding accident. Instead of giving up all hope of ever being able to live a meaningful life again, he dedicated his remaining years to aid scientific research and advocacy for people living with spinal cord injuries. Though Reeve passed away in 2004, his legacy and foundation lives on with his son.

What is certain is that an optimistic attitude will, at the very least, make your situation more bearable. For example, developing a sense of control will motivate you to keep fighting your illness. Take an active role in your treatment: inform yourself about the pros and cons of different therapies so that you can participate in decisions as a partner with your doctor, rather than feeling helpless as a patient. Focus on the things you can control. Although you are unable to do anything about the fact that you or a family member has developed a serious illness, you do have control over such matters as the way you spend your time and where you go for support.

Investigate complementary therapies to pursue alongside your core treatment. You may find relaxation methods, such as meditation, visualization, yoga, and massage particularly useful, as they will help you to

VISUALIZE A HEALING RIVER

Guided visualization is a highly versatile meditation method. You can use the following script to picture healing forces at work in your body—this may help you to cope with a painful treatment, such as chemotherapy. To allow you to focus completely on your visualization, it is a good idea to record the script onto an audio device, speaking calmly and gently, with pauses after each sentence. You can create visualizations of your own to help you face any kind of challenge, not just an illness.

1. Relax by taking deep, cleansing breaths and tensing and releasing all your muscles.

2. Close your eyes and visualize the following scene: "I am standing on the bank of a river. I know that this is a healing river. I put my toes in the water—it feels warm and soothing. I walk slowly into the river, enjoying the warm, soothing water. The water is all around me now. It penetrates my skin and my muscles and enters each individual cell, bringing with it a wonderful healing energy. This healing energy knows exactly where to go in my body to cleanse me. It washes away all sickness and restores me to health. I have a deep knowledge that I am well. I watch my illness flow away downstream. I wade back to the bank and emerge feeling healthy and whole."

3. Take a few moments to linger by the healing river before opening your eyes.

control stress and anxiety, which interfere with the healing process.

Carrying around the knowledge that you or a family member is ill can be exhausting, so to give yourself an occasional respite from the reality of your situation, designate an illness-free zone in your home. Listen to music there, or focus your mind completely on a craft or hobby that you enjoy. If you find that your mind wanders back to the illness, tell yourself, "This is an illness-free zone—I will have plenty of time to think about that illness later."

When you do let yourself think about the disease, ask yourself whether there could be any positive meaning for it. You will probably find it hard to see any meaning at all in your illness, least of all a positive one. However, some people who are forced to face their mortality by a serious —or even terminal—illness report that this experience inspires them to put right unresolved conflicts; others appreciate for the first time the preciousness of life, which makes them value every moment of the rest of their lives.

Any positive meaning is likely to reveal itself to you only gradually as you come to terms with your diagnosis. Don't compel yourself, or let anyone else compel you, to "put a brave face" on things. Allowing for emotional expression is healthy, so don't deny your anger, sadness, or fear. Instead, share your feelings honestly with people who can empathize with you. If your friends and family are finding it difficult to know how to treat you, tell them directly—but not accusingly—what you want from them. You might also consider joining a support group. Wherever you find them, you should surround yourself with optimistic people who can help you deal with this challenging time.

SEEKING HELP FROM YOUR FRIENDS AND FAMILY

One of the many difficulties in facing a serious diagnosis is dealing with your friends and family. Some people may avoid you because they don't know what to say to you. Others are willing to spend time with you but their negative attitude demoralizes you. It is often up to you to take control by letting people know how you want to be treated. You might like to give the following list to your friends and family members or adapt it to suit your needs.

If you are wondering what you can do to help me, here are some suggestions:

- Call me and ask me how I am doing and whether I would like some company.
- Ask me what I would like from you in terms of support and encouragement.
- Tell me that everything is going to be OK and that you will stick with me throughout.
- Listen to me when I tell you how I am feeling.
- Share your feelings with me about how my illness is affecting you.

- Tell me what is going on in your life so I can stay connected to you.
- Bring some laughter into my life: tell me jokes or share a video, a song, or something to read.

DEALING WITH PAIN

We all have to put up with pain from time to time. However, pain can be particularly daunting if it is associated with a chronic condition, such as fibromyalgia, a grueling cancer treatment, such as chemotherapy, an injury, or a surgical procedure. It is in situations such as these that an optimistic attitude is invaluable, helping you to treat your hardship as a challenge and to find a means of gaining control over it. By actively seeking ways to combat your pain, you will reduce the feelings of anxiety that it is likely to create. This will help your body to fight back: anxiety disrupts your sleep—deep sleep is required to support your immune system and to enable your body to produce GH, a hormone that helps wounds to heal.

The most useful thing you can do to gain control over your pain experience and reduce your anxiety toward it is to understand what is causing it. This will demystify your situation, making it less frightening and more bearable. For example, in a study by health psychologists R. P. Pinto and J. G. Hollandsworth, children who watched a video explaining the surgery they were about to undergo reported feeling less pain and recovered sooner than children undergoing the same procedure who did not see the video.

Understand your condition by researching it in books and magazines and via the internet, and write down questions to ask your doctor as they occur to you. Record the specific details of your own pain experience by keeping a health diary. This may help you to identify factors, such as diet, exercise, stress, or sleep, that exacerbate or alleviate your symptoms.

Another way to reduce your anxiety is to create guided imagery specifically to control your perception of pain. For example, you might write a script in which you lock your pain away. Picture yourself lifting your pain out of your body and shutting it in a chest or a vault that no one can ever open. As you walk away, notice how light and unburdened you feel. Keep these feelings with you to inspire you when the going is tough.

TAKING A LAUGHTER CURE

You probably don't need scientific research to tell you that laughing makes you feel good, but such research exists if you want it. Laughter has been shown to boost your immune system by increasing your level of T cells, whose function it is to defend you against infection. Laughter is exercise for your insides—other studies have shown that after a good bout of laughter, your muscles loosen up and your heart rate and blood pressure are lowered, leaving you feeling relaxed, calm, and positive.

Some people consciously use laughter as a therapy. Journalist and author Norman Cousins described in his book *Anatomy of an Illness* (1979) how he immersed himself in funny books and movies to help him recover from the degenerative rheumatic condition ankylosing spondylitis. The exercise below suggests specific ways of incorporating laughter into your day, but you can boost your laughter quotient almost imperceptibly through numerous light-hearted interactions with your family, friends and coworkers—or even with strangers in the grocery store. Develop a keen eye for the absurd. You'll find that it's never far from view. Instead of letting minor mishaps or petty regulations annoy you, look for the funny side and, when you've found it, laugh.

A merry heart does good like a medicine.

Proverbs 17:22

LOOK FOR LAUGHTER IN THE EVERYDAY

You can incorporate laughter into your day by actively seeking out humor. What tickles your funny bone? Is it found in old movies, stand-up comedy, a favorite sitcom? Whatever it is, indulge yourself. Here are three separate suggestions to include in your personal prescription for laughter. Take your medicine as often as required. You can't overdose on laughter.

1. Form a laughter club. This is a group of people who get together for the sole purpose of laughing. Ideally, arrange to meet each day for twenty minutes. Members stand in a circle, an appointed person starts the laughter, and everyone else joins in.

2. Use your commuting time to amuse yourself. If you find yourself getting stressed during your journey to or from work or school, listen to some comedy on your phone.

3. Create a "giggle trunk" for your school or your home and fill it with things that make you laugh. You might include items that make you look ridiculous, such as funny glasses, a clown nose, or a wild hat. Or you might throw in a book of jokes or cartoons. Particularly effective are photos or notes to remind you and your friends of funny situations that you've encountered together. When the mood strikes, break open the trunk, put on that silly hat, or tell that story, and just wait for the others to start giggling.

AGING WITH ATTITUDE

What words do you associate with getting older? Wisdom? Senility? Illness? Experience? What many of us don't realize is that our attitudes about aging influence our health and well-being in old age, and even our life expectancy—a compelling example of the self-fulfilling prophecy in action. Researchers from Yale University found that retired people who considered themselves to be as energetic, happy, hopeful, and useful as they were when they were younger lived more than seven years longer than those who reported more negative perceptions of aging. As a single factor, positive self-perception of aging had a greater effect on life expectancy than any one of the conventional health measures, such as blood pressure, cholesterol level, weight, and frequency of exercise.

It is important to realize now how much influence you will have over your aging process. Exercising regularly helps to improve your mood and counteract loss of muscle tone, lung capacity, and bone mass. You should also exercise your mind. Mental stimulation often comes as a matter of course in our working lives, but in retirement we may have to seek it out. You could read books to boost your concentration levels, do quizzes to test your recall, or tackle crosswords to flex your problem-solving skills—it doesn't matter, just so long as you don't let your brain get flabby. Don't make the mistake of perceiving old age as a time when you've got nothing left to offer or look forward to.

Involve yourself in your community—for example, by doing volunteer work or raising money for a charity whose work you admire or by getting involved with local government or a political organization. You could also try more personal pursuits like learning to paint, writing a book, or studying for a new degree. A sense of challenge fuels our enjoyment of life. Remember also that older people have accumulated much wisdom, which can be of benefit to younger people as they face problems similar to ones that older people have had to overcome. Be available to hear what older people have to say.

OPTIMISM AND YOUR MENTAL HEALTH

Mental health is an expression of how we feel about ourselves, other people, and our ability to meet the demands of life. Positive mental health helps us to maintain fulfilling relationships, to be productive, to adapt to change, and to cope with adversity.

In this chapter, we will learn how to maintain our mental health in the best possible state, by such means as being hopeful, finding peace of mind, and entering the "zone." Although an optimistic attitude will go a long way toward protecting your mental health, there may still be times when you are vulnerable to stress, anxiety, or depression. However, even then, as we will see, it's not too late for optimism to help you fight back and reverse the self-defeating thought patterns characteristic of these conditions. Remember: it is not what happens to you that affects your mental health, but the way you perceive what happens to you.

OPTIMIZING YOUR MENTAL HEALTH

Just like our physical health, it is easy to take mental health for granted: we focus on it only if something goes wrong. However, applying the following optimistic principles to our mental health can help us to maintain it in the best shape possible.

Express your emotions. The ability to express your feelings is crucial to positive mental health—it is emotional intelligence in action. Laugh, cry, be angry, be joyful. If we stifle our feelings, it makes it hard for people to relate to us. However, try to manage fear, anxiety, and guilt: an excess of these emotions will not serve you well. Use your journal to identify negative emotions and to understand why you are feeling them.

Live a life of purpose. Meaningful activity gives you a reason to get out of bed every day. A great deal of satisfaction can be gained from doing what you were meant to do in life; otherwise we are likely to feel bored, frustrated, and unfulfilled.

Love and be loved. Lasting, loving relationships foster a sense of belonging and a system of mutual support, which promote positive mental health. Discussing our concerns with close friends often helps us to put our problems into perspective and to find ways to deal with them. And empathizing with your friends' problems gives you the satisfaction of helping someone else, as well as stopping you from becoming preoccupied with your own worries. In order to become close to other people, we need to accept ourselves—it is difficult to love people who do not believe that they are worthy of love.

Accept yourself. Let go of the tyranny of perfectionism and negative self-talk. Accepting yourself does not mean that you can't improve and grow. It just means that you already see yourself as a worthwhile person. Everything that you become from now on is a bonus, so celebrate your achievements, rather than dwelling on your mistakes.

Be flexible. Our lives are constantly changing, often in ways that we can't control. What we can do—and what we must do if we are to thrive rather than just survive— is to accept new circumstances and adapt to them. It is perfectly normal to fear the unknown. However, if we trust in our ability to handle change and are open to new experiences, we can overcome our fear.

Find the balance. Prioritizing the demands placed upon us and allotting time accordingly helps us to minimize the distressing feeling of being pulled in many directions at the same time. Finding balance gives you precious time: time with family and friends, time alone, time to study, time to play.

The happiness of your life depends on the quality of your thoughts.

Marcus Aurelius
(AD 121–180)

OVERCOMING DEPRESSION

Most of us have come into contact with depression, directly or indirectly. Because depression is associated with pessimism and apathy, sufferers find it difficult to believe they can do anything to get better. However, in this section we will explore the many practical steps you can take to overcome depression.

We often use the word "depression" casually. We say "I'm so depressed" when really we mean we're disappointed, anxious, or sad. What differentiates clinical depression from a depressed mood is how long the experience lasts and how deeply it affects you. A clinically depressed person typically experiences at least three of the following symptoms during the same two-week period:

- Persistent sadness
- Loss of interest in things that he or she usually considers important
- Eating more or less than usual
- Sleeping more or less than usual
- Inability to concentrate or to remember things

- Lack of physical energy
- Deep, generalized pessimism
- Feelings of worthlessness
- Unwarranted feelings of guilt
- Thoughts of death or suicide

Take action now if you think that you might be suffering from depression: contact your doctor or mental health care provider. A variety of factors can contribute to depression. It can have a genetic component, a predisposition that runs in families. There is a link between chronic stress and depression. For example, the prolonged stress related to an unsustainable course load or the death of a loved one can trigger a depressive episode. Some people experience depression in reaction to a major change in their lives, such as moving to a new area or a divorce in the family. Depression is also associated with certain medical conditions, such as hypothyroidism.

Your chances of developing depression are increased if these factors are combined with learned helplessness, which is closely associated with a pessimistic explanatory style. Pessimists blame themselves for negative events and feel powerless to better their situation—it isn't difficult to see how this attitude might contribute to the symptoms of depression.

In dealing with depression, you should try to take action early on. Be aware of changes in your mood and use your journal to explore what is happening to you whenever your mood drops. Don't worry about sentence structure or grammar; honest, uninhibited expression of your emotions matters more than elegant prose. The act of writing helps you to feel in control, which is the opposite of learned helplessness and one of the hallmarks of the optimist. Analyzing your feelings in this way can also help you to find a more positive interpretation.

Exercise is an effective, proven method of dealing with mild to moderate depression, and regular exercise can also act as a preventive measure for people who are not currently depressed but who are predisposed to the condition. Starting a walking program is a good option, as it gives you the added bonus of a refreshing change of scenery, although any type of activity will produce benefits. Write down your exercise goals in your journal: perhaps thirty minutes of walking each day. If the prospect of walking on your own does not inspire you, join a walking group. Alternatively, practice the "five-minute rule" on the days when you don't feel like walking. Just go walking for five minutes and then turn back if you want to. Chances are you will keep going!

There are numerous alternative therapies that you might consider for treating mild depression. These include therapeutic massage, acupuncture, meditation, and homeopathy, including Saint John's wort capsules. If you are interested in pursuing any of these therapies, always consult a reputable practitioner.

If, having tried a variety of self-help coping strategies, your depression persists, counseling may be a sensible next step. Even if you continue to function at work and home, depression is not good for your health and should be dealt with.

Your counselor, in conjunction with your doctor, may recommend the use of antidepressants, which are a viable and sometimes necessary option for people with moderate

HERBS AND SPICES

There are times when the natural world can be helpful to ease stress or brighten a mood. Some alternative therapies and medicines recommend exploring the possible uses of herbs and spices beyond being tasty seasonings for your food. For example, ginger is often recommended to help settle your stomach. And whether sage, mint, lavender, or even pine needles have any specific healing properties, taking a moment to breathe in their aromas can be a great way to pause your mind, briefly focus on one sensation (scent), and enjoy their fragrances.

The same can be said for using herbal teas. Does chamomile really relax you, or is it the act of sitting down and talking a little time to enjoy a hot beverage that's doing the trick? Either way, it can be a soothing ritual to help you unwind.

There has been more concrete evidence that St. John's wort can be helpful in treating mild depression. Before taking any size dose, though, be sure to discuss this option with a parent and doctor to understand its possible effects more fully.

to severe depression who have tried other methods without success. Research suggests that a combination of medication and counseling is the most effective treatment for severe depression.

MANAGING STRESS

We live in a world in which we take stress for granted. Too many deadlines, not enough time, too many interruptions, not enough quiet, too much technology, not enough simplicity, too much work to do, not enough leisure time . . . and the list goes on. Although we may not always be able to avoid the things that cause us stress, we can influence how we respond to them. But before we look at how we can manage our stress, we first need to understand how stress works.

When you encounter a situation that you perceive as threatening in some way, your brain sends signals to your body along the sympathetic nervous system. Your body prepares to deal with the threat by releasing the hormones cortisol and adrenaline (epinephrine), which speed up your heart and your breathing, slow down your digestion, increase your blood pressure, and cause your muscles to tense. This is the so-called fight or flight mechanism. After the threat has passed, the parasympathetic system reverses the fight or flight responses.

We need a certain amount of stress in our lives to

ACTIVATE YOUR RELAXATION RESPONSE

Meditation is a relaxation technique that involves focusing your attention on a single thing, such as an object, a word or phrase, your breathing, or an everyday task. The following meditation is designed to elicit your relaxation response. Practice it every day during quiet moments, so that it comes readily when you feel overwhelmed by stress.

1. Sit quietly in a comfortable chair with your back well supported and both feet flat on the floor. Close your eyes and focus on your breathing as you breathe in and out. Imagine that with each inhale you are breathing in positive energy and that with each exhale you are breathing out negative thoughts or emotions.

2. When you have become focused on your breathing, silently repeat a short word—for example "one" or "calm" —on each exhale.

3. Don't worry if your mind wanders. Just let your stray thoughts pass across your mind without trying to chase them away. Gently refocus on your breath and start the process all over again.

4. To begin with, meditate for five minutes, then build up gradually to ten or twenty minutes. At the end of your meditation, take a moment to reorient yourself back to the outside world. Focus on how positive and relaxed you feel. Take these feelings with you as you go about the rest of your day.

stop us from becoming bored and to enable us to do our best in "performance situations," such as giving a speech or taking a test. However, stress becomes a problem when our fight or flight mechanism is permanently switched on, preventing the parasympathetic system from bringing our bodies back into balance. This imbalance plays havoc with our physical and emotional well-being, triggering a chain of symptoms, such as muscle pain, insomnia, fatigue, sadness, heart palpitations, heartburn, diarrhea, nausea, anxiety, teeth grinding, and headaches. In the long term, chronically elevated levels of cortisol and adrenaline can compromise your immune system and predispose you to heart disease and strokes.

Anything can be a source of stress to you if you perceive it as such. By the same token, if you can manage your perception of potentially stressful situations, you can stop stress from escalating out of control and affecting your health. As optimists perceive events in the most positive way possible, it follows that they tend to be particularly adept at resisting the negative effects of stress.

A major piece of research conducted by the psychologist Suzanne Kobasa in the 1970s underlines the importance of a positive attitude in managing stress. She studied a group of business executives over the course of eight years and observed that the executives who were best able to cope with work pressures possessed a set of traits she described as hardiness. Hardiness has much in common with optimism—its main components are a sense of commitment to involve oneself in meaningful activity; an internal locus of control over events; and the ability to approach a situation as a challenge rather than a problem.

By developing an optimistic attitude, using the techniques presented throughout this book, it follows that you will find fewer situations stressful. For example, seeking positive meaning in ostensibly negative events enables you to stay committed to your goals despite any setbacks. Making a plan to face up to a fear gives you control over something that previously controlled you. Using creative techniques to overcome an obstacle in your way helps you to rise to the challenge.

However, even optimists feel the strain from time to time. When you are under stress, the challenge is to switch off your fight or flight mechanism and to proceed to allow your parasympathetic system to induce what the mind–body medicine pioneer Herbert Benson termed the relaxation response. The problem is that, whereas the fight or flight mechanism is triggered automatically, we often have to remind our bodies to deploy the relaxation response.

One approach is to do some exercise, to provide an outlet for pent-up adrenaline. It doesn't have to be particularly strenuous—even a brisk walk would help to dispel some tension and to give you some respite from the source of your stress. With its emphasis on regulating breathing and relaxing tense muscles, yoga is another good option. You can also reduce your adrenaline level by cutting down your caffeine intake.

Meditation is a great method for slowing down your thoughts and your breathing, enabling you to replace an agitated state of mind with calmness. Similar to meditation, autogenic training involves projecting a sense of ease onto tense parts of your body. Lie down for ten minutes and focus on each tense area in turn. Say to yourself, for example, "My arm feels heavy." Sense your previously knotted arm muscles feeling relaxed and heavy. Keep repeating the affirmation "My arm feels heavy" for about a minute before moving on to the next part of your body.

"Control and change" is a means of identifying your stressors and deciding how to stop them from being stressful to you. First, make a list in your journal of the things that you find stressful. Next, divide the stressors into two groups: those you can change and those you can't. For each stressor in the first group, write down what you are going to do to change it. For example, if the untidiness of your room is making you edgy, you might plan out a weekly housework routine. For stressors beyond your control, write down a way of avoiding them or changing your attitude to them. Perhaps you are stressed by the traffic on your way to and from school—you might use your commuting time positively, perhaps to prepare for the next phase of your day. Remember the Serenity Prayer: "Grant me the serenity to accept the things I can't change, the courage to change the things I can, and the wisdom to know the difference."

LIVING WITH HOPE

Hope is the device that optimists use to propel themselves into the future. The psychologist Charles R. Snyder defines hope as the belief that "you have both the will and the way to accomplish your goals." Hope is closely linked to optimism: if we are able to explain past or current events optimistically, it follows that we will feel hopeful about the future. Conversely, hopelessness or despair about the future is one of the most destructive features of pessimism and depression. It is during the tough times—when we are most vulnerable to feelings of despair—that the benefits of hopefulness are most apparent.

Research has shown the value of hope in the face of adversity. In one study, led by Dr. Tim Elliott, an expert in rehabilitation psychology, a group of people paralyzed by spinal-cord injury were tested for hopefulness. Over time, the ones who were found to be most hopeful were less depressed and more mobile than the others. The actor Christopher Reeve, who made incredible progress after having been paralyzed by a spinal-cord injury, observed that hope is a choice. Choosing to be hopeful when it feels as if everything is going against you is not easy, but it is possible. One way to cultivate hope is to seek inspiration from the examples of people, such as Christopher Reeve, who have had the courage to carry on in the face of hardship. Don't forget that we can all find such examples in our own personal history. Think back to times when you were at your lowest and seek comfort and strength from the fact that you overcame them. Time heals: what seems unendurable today will never feel quite as bad in the future.

Visualize a compelling future for yourself, so that you look ahead in anticipation rather than trepidation. Where do you want to be in, say, a year's time? Write down any steps you can take to achieve this position. Whom can you ask for help? Even if some aspects of your future are beyond your control, knowing what you want to happen, hoping that it will happen, and doing what you can to make it happen will maximize your chances of success.

When the unthinkable happens, the lighthouse is hope. Once we choose hope, everything is possible.

Christopher Reeve
(1952–2004)

FINDING PEACE OF MIND

Peace of mind is a precious sense of contentment. If you look for it, you won't find it; it only comes to you when your mind is still and empty of negative emotions, such as guilt, bitterness, and anxiety, which can dominate our thoughts and weaken our energy and morale. So, to find peace of mind, we must first let go of these emotions.

One of the reasons optimists are so good at finding peace of mind is that they remember the positive aspects of past events and overlook the negatives. They also take action to resolve differences with other people rather than letting bad feeling linger, escalate, and eat away at their peace of mind. If you have been hurt by someone else's actions, practice forgiveness—not for the other person's benefit, but for your own. To forgive is to let go of the bitterness we feel each time we think about what happened. Similarly, if you know that you have hurt someone else, try to repair the damage or atone for your actions. Often, taking the initiative to communicate with the other person is the biggest step in healing emotional wounds.

As well as thinking too much about the past, thinking too much about the future can disrupt your peace of mind. Anxiety about the future can take over, affecting our decisions and our enjoyment of life. Rather than fret about what may or may not lie ahead, try to create an inspiring vision of your future.

One solution to avoid regret about the past and fear of the future is to spend time living "mindfully" in the present. Associated with meditation, mindfulness comes from the Buddhist tradition. It involves focusing all of your attention on what you are currently doing, so that your mind becomes still.

GOING ON A RETREAT

In this hyperactive world, there may be times when you need to separate yourself physically from your day-to-day activities in order to find stillness. Going on a retreat is one way to take this step back, to follow the advice of the Indian politician Indira Gandhi: "You must learn to be still in the midst of activity, and to be vibrantly alive in repose."

Nothing rivals a personal retreat for promoting peace of mind. If you have no experience of retreats, a good place to start is to attend an organized one, perhaps based around a theme, such as discovering yourself through art or listening to your inner voice.

However, you don't need to go on an organized retreat in order to enjoy the benefits of being still: you can design your own. Your retreat can be as long or as short as you like —even an hour's walk can help to still your thoughts. Use your journal to plan what you can do during your retreat to create peace of mind. You might start by taking a long bath to symbolize washing away the cares of the outside world. Just as important as what you do during your retreat is what you don't do. The key is to avoid the things that make you agitated. For example, if you are sensitive to caffeine, cut out tea or coffee the day before and during your retreat, don't be ruled by the clock, and stay away from the news.

IMMERSING YOURSELF

Athletes go there, so do artists of all types. You have probably been there at different times. It's what many people call the zone and what the leading authority on the subject Mihaly Csikszentmihalyi (pronounced "CHEEK-sent-me-high-ee") calls flow. When Tiger Woods plays golf well, he does not think about the crowds, the opponents, or the money at stake, he focuses exclusively on each shot. Flow is a state of total concentration in which you are so intent on what you are doing that you are oblivious to what is going on around you.

When you are involved in an activity that produces the flow experience, your worries leave you. Time flies and you lose awareness of yourself: your body and mind work in harmony. You may not feel particularly happy during the experience itself, especially if the activity is an arduous one, such as running or swimming. However, once you have finished, you feel a great sense of satisfaction, high self-esteem, and competence. Research has also shown that people who report experiencing flow on a regular basis feel that their lives are meaningful.

The root understanding of the word ecstasy—"to stand outside"—comes to me in those moments when I am immersed so deeply in the act of thinking and writing that everything else . . . falls away.

bell hooks (1952–)

We often experience flow when engaged in sports and creative pursuits, such as painting, crafts, and music. However, flow is created by how you go about an activity and so can be found anywhere. Indeed, you will feel happier if you are able to create flow in a wide variety of pursuits. If you rely exclusively on one activity, such as school, for your flow experiences, there is a danger that you will become obsessed with that activity and neglect other important areas of your life.

Although the ability to enter the flow lies within you, you can't force yourself into this state of mind. Rather like attempting to get to sleep, the harder you try, the harder it becomes. However, you can create the conditions to make flow likely to occur. For example, slow down your thoughts in readiness for the task you are to undertake —perhaps by meditating or taking deep, slow breaths. Embarking on an activity in an agitated mood makes it very hard to immerse yourself in the task at hand.

Choose an activity that presents a realistic challenge to your abilities and allows you to aim for clearly defined goals. If you are faced with too great a challenge, you will feel anxious and demoralized; not enough of a challenge and you will be bored. As you improve in the task, raise your expectations, so that you are always aiming for a goal just above your current skill level. Flow is also likely if you do something that provides immediate feedback. For example, every time they move to a new handhold or foothold, experienced rock climbers can tell immediately whether they are making the right moves.

OPTIMISM IN ACTION

In the first four chapters of this book, we explored the theory of optimism, how to acquire it, and how it benefits your physical and mental health. In this chapter, we will look in more detail at how to use and share your optimism skills in the most familiar life contexts, at school and at home.

Discover how to build and maintain a positive, supportive, and understanding relationship, how to share the precious gift of optimism with your family, and how to make your home a fun, happy place for you and your family to live. You will also learn how to lend your optimism skills to friends who are in need of a positive outlook. Finally, we will see how you can apply a "can do" attitude to your studying or after-school job, to ensure that it is as fulfilling as possible.

OPTIMISM AND SUCCESS

It is firmly accepted by Robert's teammates that his talent for basketball is superior to that of another teammate, Brian. Yet Brian is a more successful athlete—more points per game than Robert. Brian is an upbeat guy who is known for his persistence when faced with a scoring drought; he just keeps trying, and eventually he gets back on the scoreboard.

This imaginary scenario conveys what countless studies have proved: you can't succeed with ability alone. What makes the difference is optimism. In this section, we will take a tour of some of the research that has been conducted into the benefits of optimism in various real-life settings. No matter what situation you are in, qualities such as emotional intelligence, self-esteem, and resilience will help you to succeed.

A study of first-year college students found that those with an optimistic explanatory style for negative events (it's not my fault; it won't last; it doesn't affect anything else) tended to have higher grades than students of similar ability who had a pessimistic explanatory style. The researchers also noted that the optimistic students set more specific goals and were more likely to seek academic counseling than the pessimistic students. These two "take action" factors were both felt to contribute to the success of the optimistic students.

The world of sports, with its precise performance measures, provides an excellent arena for demonstrating the power of optimism. Time and again, teams and individual competitors with optimistic attributional styles outperform pessimistic rivals of similar or greater natural ability. In one study, swimmers competed in an event swimming their best stroke. After the event, all swimmers were deliberately misinformed that their performance had been below average. They were asked to swim the same event again. Optimistic swimmers did as well as the first time, whereas pessimistic swimmers swam more slowly the second time.

No empowerment is so effective as self-empowerment. In this world, the optimists have it, not because they are always right, but because they are positive. Even when wrong, they are positive, and that is the way of achievement.

David Landes
(1924–2013)

THE OPTIMISTIC COUPLE

If you wanted to be pessimistic about the future of romantic relationships (married or otherwise), you could do worse than quote the rising divorce rate, which, in some countries, is now as high as 50 percent for new marriages. However, taking the optimistic view, if many

marriages end in divorce, just as many—if not more—
are destined to last. Not surprisingly, much research has
been undertaken to try to understand what makes some
relationships last and others fail. These studies have found
that, as in every other aspect of our lives, optimism has a
significant part to play in creating happy, fulfilling, long-
lasting relationships.

A key finding is that optimists not only explain their
own actions in a positive way, they also come up with
positive interpretations of their partner's behavior. For
example, you might observe your parents. One partner
walks through the front door at the end of the day and yells
"I can't stand it when you leave your shoes right where I can
trip over them!" The other partner might react by thinking:
"Wow, he/she must have had a difficult day at work."
Alternatively, they might think: "Why does he/she always
have to be in such a bad mood?"

How you explain your partner's behavior is
an indication of your overall happiness with the
relationship. The first explanation is more indicative of
a happy relationship than the second because it involves
attributing the other person's negative behavior to an
external factor, in this case work, rather than to an
intrinsic character flaw, as in the second explanation.
Of course, one should be careful not to confuse negative
behavior with abusive behavior. If something always
seems wrong or sad or dangerous, this might be a very
unhealthy relationship. How do you interpret your

partner's actions? It might be helpful to analyze your reaction to a recent example of his or her negative behavior—perhaps he or she acted angrily or forgot to do something important. In your journal, describe the situation and how you felt about it. Answer the following questions: Do you blame your partner entirely for what happened or can you see mitigating factors? Do you see the behavior as being typical of your partner or as an isolated reaction to a specific set of circumstances? Do you believe that he or she intended to speak or act this way or was it an accident? Do you feel that this event has an impact on your relationship as a whole or are the repercussions confined to the episode in question? In your view, does this type of situation happen often or rarely? You will probably have guessed that the first option in each case is the pessimistic interpretation and the second the optimistic. In the short term, this method gives you a quick diagnosis of your style of interpreting your partner's behavior. However, particularly if your interpretation was on the pessimistic side, you can also use the exercise on an ongoing basis as a means of empathizing with your partner, in order consciously to view their negative behavior in a more positive light.

As we have seen, an optimistic attitude does not have to be grounded in reality. Just as happy couples downplay the other person's negative aspects, they also exaggerate their partner's positive behavior and believe that it is characteristic of them. How do couples maintain these "positive illusions" about one another? One way to understand your family dynamics is to reframe your parent's weaknesses as strengths. For example: "When she pays so much attention to the details of every little thing, it makes me crazy, but I also recognize that it helps her to be a good mother."

An important differentiator between happy and unhappy relationships is the way in which partners interact with each other. Dr. John Gottman, author of *The Seven Principles for Making Marriage Work* (1999) and *The Relationship Cure* (2001), asserts that he can predict with 91 percent accuracy the couples who will stay together just by observing how they interact. He focuses on how, and how often, each partner "bids" for emotional connection with the other and how he or she responds. Bids come in many forms, verbal and nonverbal: a question, a facial expression, a touch, a sigh—any gesture or comment that says "I want to be connected to you." People who stay married have at least five times as many positive interactions as negative interactions and they make significantly more bids to each other than unhappy couples.

Responses to a bid fall into three categories: "turning toward," "turning against," and "turning away." A turning-toward response is a positive reaction to a bid. You smile at your partner; they smile back. These interactions go into a "goodwill bank account," which the couple can draw upon on the inevitable occasions when conflict does arise. When turning-toward couples disagree, they use humor, affection, and respect to stay connected and avoid the onslaught of negative feelings that cause relationships to dissolve.

Gottman characterizes a turning-against response as a belligerent, argumentative, or sarcastic counter to a bid. You smile at your partner; they snap back, "What?" When one partner often responds in this way, the other tends to suppress his or her feelings and in the majority of cases the relationship does not last.

A turning-away response involves one partner ignoring the other's bid. A question goes unanswered, a display of affection is brushed away, or a conversation fizzles out because of comments or body language that signal lack of interest. Again, a pattern of turning away often results in divorce.

We don't always realize how our words and actions make our partner feel. Although you can't control his or her feelings, you can regulate your own emotions and behavior so that you turn toward your partner as often as possible. Pay attention to your partner's body language. If he or she seems unhappy, ask yourself how you would like your partner to treat you if you were unhappy and act accordingly. If he or she is irritable, try to rein in the irritation you may feel in response. Rather than letting bad feelings linger or escalate, you can acknowledge what you did that upset your partner, apologize, and if he or she has upset you, explain why you feel upset.

CREATE "COUPLE TIME"

Relationships require an investment of a precious resource, something that we are always struggling to find more of—time. This exercise suggests ways in which you and your partner can reserve time together, simply enjoying each other's company or collaborating in fulfilling activities.

1. Schedule a regular time together, such as a Friday night or a Sunday morning. Make it a ritual. If you keep to a regular time, you are unlikely to schedule something else in that time slot by mistake: "Lunch on Tuesday? I can't. I always eat lunch with my husband on Tuesdays."

2. Taking action is good for your mood. Sharing an experience with your partner is also good for your relationship. It doesn't matter what you do, it's the sharing that counts: perhaps you could exercise together or join a club together.

3. Television can be an intimacy thief, stealing what precious time we do have. If at all possible, create a television-free zone in your home that is set up for conversations, not distractions.

4. Take a half-hour walk with your partner. Use this time to reconnect with each other, to share concerns. If it

has been so long since you and your partner have spent time alone that you don't know what to talk about, tell him or her what you think are the positive aspects of your relationship. That's always a great place to start.

THE OPTIMISTIC STUDENT

Teaching your peers or younger siblings to be optimists is the most valuable, life-enhancing thing you can do for them. Optimistic children are more likely to be happy, healthy, to have friends, and to achieve success at school— important stepping-stones to becoming caring, productive adults.

In most cases, a child's style of explaining good and bad events, which sets the stage for optimism or pessimism, develops gradually up to the age of about nine or ten, by which time it is well defined.

Babies and toddlers have no concept of success or failure. They are motivated simply by the process of learning something new. At around two years of age, children become aware of their parents evaluating their behavior, which makes them seek praise and recognize disapproval. From the age of three, children begin to set their own standards of success and failure and to appraise their performance independently of other people's judgments.

There are two paths along which a child's explanatory style might develop: toward mastery or toward learned helplessness.

Children who are mastery oriented believe that their successes come from their own ability and effort and their failures from external factors. They are confident that if they try hard enough, they will overcome challenges. They also believe that they can improve their abilities by trying harder. Because they feel they can control their environment, mastery-oriented children take pleasure in their activities and are motivated to persist despite setbacks. These children gladly face new challenges, which helps them develop their problem-solving and coping skills.

Children with a learned-helplessness orientation often attribute success to luck and failure to low ability. They operate on the assumption that ability is a stable characteristic that can't be changed. They don't feel that they can improve by trying harder, so they are likely to give up, leading to increasingly low expectations of success. Pessimism develops because they believe that they can't control or change the outcome of a situation. They derive their motivation to do well from a desire to avoid criticism. Using the perceived judgments of other people to guide their behavior causes them to lose touch with the positive feelings that come with achievement and sharpens the pain of failure.

As with adults, children who explain their world in a pessimistic manner are at risk for depression. For example, approximately 3 percent of children in the United States struggle with depression at any one time. Recognizing the signs is not always easy. Children who are depressed do not necessarily look or act sad: aggression and irritability are more common symptoms. Any marked and persistent change in your child's behavior warrants concern and intervention. Always err on the side of caution.

The most important tool that you have at your disposal is your own attitude. Do you refer to the positive side of life more than the negative? Do you come up with positive explanations when things go wrong? Share your positive self-talk with your peers or siblings so that they can use your optimistic thoughts as an example. Tell them stories about difficulties that you have overcome.

In order to strengthen a child's sense of personal responsibility for his or her successes, praise effort rather than ability. Effort is something that can be controlled directly and immediately, whereas ability can only be developed over time as a result of effort. So, for example, if your friend gets a good grade at school, say "You worked really hard on that project" instead of "Look how smart you are."

Use descriptive praise to help a child make his or her own evaluations and learn to praise himself or herself. Descriptive praise makes it clear to a child what he or she has achieved. For example, if you were babysitting, saying: "You've brushed your teeth and put on your pajamas—thanks for listening to me" rather than "What a good little boy you are for listening to me."

The second version imposes your evaluation on the child, which may hamper his ability to make his own judgments. Similarly, when a child shows you his or her latest artistic creation, you might try saying "Tell me about your

SHOW A CHILD A POSITIVE FUTURE

Children have to tackle all kinds of new challenges—for example, starting school, taking exams, and making friends. They may be daunted by the prospect of entering unknown territory. The following exercise shows how you can be hopeful about the future by helping yourself to visualize what you want to happen and identify what you can do to make it happen.

1. If you're facing a new challenge, find a quiet time to discuss it with a parent. Share how you feel about the upcoming event. Let's say it's the end of summer, and a new school year is about to start. Try to visualize the first day. How do you want things to go? How do you want to feel when you come home at the end of the day?

2. Ask yourself what you would like to achieve at school in the coming year. Perhaps you want to do well in a certain class or take up a musical instrument or a sport. Set your own goals—don't let your parents do it for you. Ask for support in your ideas and ask yourself what you can do to make things happen the way you want them to.

3. Remind yourself that your parent will love and support you regardless of what happens. Your aim should be to take away the external pressure of feeling you have to do well to earn their love. It's important that your primary motivation should be internal.

picture" instead of telling the child "What a good artist you are."

Do not reward indiscriminately. Rewarding everything children do sets them up always to expect external motivation, which decreases the intrinsic satisfaction they can gain purely from their own effort and achievement. Studies show that external, or extrinsic, motivators, such as money or food, are not only ineffective over the long term but are actually counterproductive. Children will lose interest and motivation when rewarded for something that they wanted to do anyway or for something that presents little or no challenge to them.

LEARN MASTERY

Your success at school and in the world is built on mastery —a belief that you can create the conditions for your success. Mastery-based learning helps you feel valued and competent—two important ingredients for creating success. Follow these steps to help cultivate a sense of mastery:

1. Mastery is developed through making decisions, so take responsibility for making your own decisions, including for the clothes you wear, activities you engage in, books you read, and so on.

2. Take opportunities to become engaged in subjects or activities that interest you. Work together with a parent to shape a project of your choice. Break the

project down into individual components, to make it easier for you to see how the successful completion of each step contributes to the success of the project as a whole.

3. Let's use the theme of making a model car as an example. Think through the steps yourself: "First we need to draw a design, then we'll have to find the materials, then decide how to put them together, and then we'll be ready to paint the car." Make as many decisions as possible about which materials to use, what color to paint the car, and so on. Do some stages on your own.

THE OPTIMISTIC FAMILY

A happy, optimistic family enriches the lives of all its members. It is within the family structure, whatever form that takes, that we first learn how to manage emotions, how to develop meaningful relationships, and how to cope with hard times. Adults, in turn, derive great happiness from a fulfilling relationship with a partner and children. Our family shapes who we are, our self-worth, and our view of the world. Optimism produces strong families in which each member enjoys the love, support, and acceptance of the others, enabling them individually and collectively to meet the challenges of life.

Many people have attempted to define the elements that make for an optimistic family. One model is known as the five Cs: commitment, connection, communication, caring, and coping.

In a strong family, each individual feels a sense of commitment to the family as a whole. They do what they can to ensure they contribute to the well-being of the other members, by sharing in the family workload, and by spending a large amount of "quality time" with their family. Although they also pursue personal goals, they believe that their family goals are more important. A committed family provides security and support for all its members. Solidify your family's commitment by having regular family meetings, planning a vacation as a family, or by working on a project together.

TAKE TIME TO PLAY

Playing together enables you to forge a strong family connection in a way that brings happiness and fulfillment to family life. The only ingredients you need to put the following exercise into practice are time and enthusiasm—family fun doesn't need to be expensive.

1. Designate at least one day each month as a special fun day for your family. If a full day is not practical because of time constraints, a half-day or a couple of hours is fine. Try to pick a fun name for these occasions.

2. Involve the whole family in the planning of your fun times together. Everyone will probably bombard you with ideas, so you might want to keep some on file for future fun days.

3. To get you started, here are a few ideas for a family fun day:
   - Do some stargazing in your backyard or from your balcony and bring along a picnic.
   - Look out for local organized events: many communities have free or inexpensive concerts or fairs that your family can enjoy together.
   - Try an afternoon or evening camping trip in your home: make a tent with sheets, bring out the sleeping bags, and at bedtime turn off the lights and read a story by flashlight.

Members of happy families build a strong **connection** with each other through family routines and traditions, such as sitting down for dinner together each evening, going for a family walk on Sunday mornings, or visiting Grandma's every Saturday. Routines and rituals provide a sense of stability in an ever-changing world. To help strengthen your family connections, start a new tradition in your family, such as a family game night, or spend individual time with your parent.

Positive communication helps to create an open family environment in which disagreements can be aired and resolved and sensitive issues discussed comfortably. Encourage honest, constructive communication in your family by ensuring that everyone's opinion is listened to and respected, children included. Ask questions in order to understand people's point of view and keep the climate positive by using humor (although not sarcasm or putdowns) and plenty of loving nonverbal communication, such as hugs and smiles. Express appreciation much more often than criticism and emphasize the areas of agreement in a conflict.

Caring is a vital element in a happy family. Family members express how much they care for each other in many ways—through respect, encouragement, acceptance, empathy, and thoughtfulness. These episodes make both giver and receiver feel good and inspire further acts of caring. Recognize your family's kindnesses by taking the time to thank each other for all the good things you have done for each other that week.

An optimistic family is just as likely as any other to undergo crises, big and small. What sets it apart is its success in coping with them. At such times, optimistic families pull together, with each member looking for ways to shoulder the collective burden. They encourage each other to hang in there and are able to point out the positives in negative situations. They can talk about a time when the crisis won't seem so overwhelming, instilling hope for a positive future.

Feelings of worth can flourish only in an atmosphere where individual differences are appreciated, mistakes are tolerated, communication is open, and rules are flexible—the kind of atmosphere that is found in a nurturing family.

Virginia Satir
(1916–1988)

HELPING OTHERS TO BE OPTIMISTIC

We come into contact with negative attitudes on a daily basis. Although we can't change other people (goodness knows, we have enough work changing ourselves), we can lend them an alternative, more optimistic perspective at those times when they are finding it hard to be positive.

When someone you care about is feeling negative in the face of a difficult situation, the most important thing you can do is listen to what he or she has to say. Allow the person to express all of his or her negative emotions without trying to talk him or her out of it. Maintain eye contact and use "minimal encouragers," such as "uh huh," "mm," or "oh," to let the other person know that you are following what he or she is saying without interrupting the flow. It is not helpful to say, "You shouldn't feel that way" or "Stop worrying, everything's fine." Appearing to trivialize the other person's reasons for feeling unhappy may give that person the impression that you don't understand or care, which will only add to his or her negative feelings.

You should also avoid the "yes, buts." We sometimes unintentionally disqualify what the other person is saying and feeling by responding in this way. For example: "Yes it's awful, but you shouldn't worry about it." Instead, it's often better just to mirror what the person has said: "You're having a tough time" or "This is really difficult for you." Although you are merely echoing his or her words, this simple act reassures that person that you empathize.

Helping someone you care about dig for the positives when he or she is up against it can redirect disaster thinking. Give the person hope by guiding his or her thoughts to a time in the future when the problem has passed. Ask: "What will you do when you don't have this problem in your life anymore?" Put the negative situation in context by helping your friend to see that even if the worst were to happen, he or she would still be OK. And point out all the things that your friend has in his or her favor.

Your friend may doubt his or her ability to tackle the problem that he or she is facing. To boost your friend's confidence, remind your friend of his or her strengths and of what he or she has achieved in the past. Perhaps he or she was struck down with a debilitating illness and had the courage to fight it and recover from it. You might ask your friend "How did you overcome that?" to trigger memories of resilience.

At times it may be appropriate to use the "it could have been worse" scenario. For example: "You had your jewelry stolen, but at least you didn't get hurt." Be careful with this approach, though. If you use it when the other person is clearly upset, you may appear unsympathetic or patronizing. Take your lead from your friend's feelings.

When someone you care about is chronically pessimistic and he or she rejects your offers of help, don't react aggressively—this may make him or her retreat further from you. Just let that person know that you are willing to listen, support, and help, if and when he or she wants you to. However, if that person carries on complaining without doing anything to improve the situation, at a certain point you may feel you have to confront him or her: "I'm listening to you talk about this problem. What's your solution?" Encourage the person struggling to express his or her feelings, but don't let the person wallow in negativity indefinitely.

The "three-complaint rule" is a method you can use among your family and friends to put a stop to unproductive complaining about minor problems. If a person complains about something three times, then he or she has either to stop talking about it or do something about it: three complaints and you're out!

WHAT'S THE WORST THAT CAN HAPPEN?

We all lose perspective when we are under pressure. A minor mishap can take on catastrophic proportions. If you see a friend going through a stressful time, one of the most helpful things you can do is sit down with your friend and show him or her that he or she can cope with even the worst outcome.

1. When someone you care about is struggling with a challenge, suggest that he or she take a break. Take that person away from his or her normal surroundings—for example, to a coffee shop or a park.

2. Ask your struggling friend to share his or her worst fears with you. For example, if he or she is trying to pass a big test, he or she may be worried that failing it means he or she will fail the class.

3. Question your friend's worst-case scenario. Remind your friend how valued he or she is. Cite examples of people who have failed a test, yet gone on to great academic success.

4. Next, even though you do not think it will happen, explore your friend's worst-case scenario.

5. Encourage your friend to focus his or her thoughts instead on the best that can happen. Ask him or her to visualize how good it will feel to succeed.

OPTIMISM IN THE OUTSIDE WORLD

An optimistic workplace is crucial to the success of any organization. Though you might be working only part-time now, it's important to learn how optimism can affect the workplace and how even you can help it become better right now. If its employees feel happy, committed, and motivated, a company is more likely to enjoy low levels of staff turnover, absenteeism and burnout, and high levels of productivity, customer satisfaction, and even profitability. Quite apart from any commercial benefits, working in an optimistic environment makes people feel good about themselves, which has a positive impact on all aspects of their lives. In this section, we will examine the factors that contribute to an optimistic workplace and what we can all do, regardless of our job title, to spread optimism in our working lives.

Towers Perrin, a human resources consulting firm, recently published the results of a study to analyze employees' feelings about their work. As well as finding a correlation between a happy workforce and a healthy balance sheet (and a dissatisfied workforce and poor financial performance), this study identified the three main elements of a positive work experience. First, a company should cultivate its employees' self-worth, by creating an environment in which they feel confident, competent, and in control of their work. Second, employees need to see how their efforts contribute to the success of the company. Finally, they need to feel appropriately recognized and rewarded for their work.

If a company demonstrates commitment to its employees, they will tend to reciprocate. There are many ways in which an employer can show how highly it values its staff, including instituting reasonable and flexible working hours, wellness programs, and subsidized social events. Even something as simple as freshening up the physical workplace by rearranging furniture or redecorating and ensuring that the work areas are safe and comfortable, conveys the message that the employer cares about the conditions in which its employees work.

Regardless of your employer's philosophy, you have the power to breed optimism in your workplace by being an attitude role model. Smile, greet people in a friendly tone of voice, and treat everyone with respect at all times. Be a good listener and don't interrupt—this will show people that you value what they have to say and will make them likely to listen to you when it's your turn.

Make positive connections with your coworkers by taking time to celebrate happy events, such as birthdays, anniversaries, and graduations. Show solidarity with people who are having a stressful time, perhaps by taking them out for lunch or a coffee or sharing a funny story. Express your appreciation when someone helps you, and praise coworkers for a job well done. Building a strong team spirit enables groups of coworkers to empathize with and support each other, which is particularly valuable when the pressure is on.

In contrast, working in a negative environment is demoralizing and alienating. Various factors may make people feel unhappy in their jobs, such as an unmanageable (or unchallenging) workload, unclear direction from senior management, and a lack of job security or satisfaction. Rampant negativity allowed to run unchecked through an organization creates a fertile breeding ground for employee burnout. Burnout is a state of physical and emotional exhaustion, the early symptoms of which may include cynicism, emotional withdrawal, lack of confidence, and irritability. In a positive workplace, someone would be likely to identify these symptoms in a coworker (because they would be so unusual) and would probably intervene. However, in a negative workplace, the signs of burnout are hard to distinguish from the prevailing mood and so may be left to develop into anxiety or depression.

If you find yourself working with a negative person, it is up to you to take action before that person's influence spreads. Negative people often do not realize that they are being negative, so the first thing you need to do is let them know what effect their attitude is having on other people. Confront them with honest, objective feedback, giving specific examples. For instance, if the person complains that all his or her coworkers are incompetent, point out how demoralizing it is for the other members of the team to hear this.

Complaining, although on the surface a negative pursuit, can be a positive force if it leads to solutions. When people complain, ask them how the situation can be improved and then involve them in implementing the change. Ask them for specific details to understand their problem and so to find a way to solve it. Taking a simple example, if someone complains that it's too noisy, ask them which specific kinds of noise they find disturbing and invite them to suggest a way of reducing the noise.

It should be noted that a workplace can be optimistic and still find room for defensive pessimism. Indeed, a company in which everyone were optimistic all the time would be destined for bankruptcy. The ability to see and plan for the worst-case scenario is an essential element in determining the success of every organization.

Like any other group of people, a workforce is a collection of diverse individuals, each with his or her own particular talents. In an optimistic workplace, these talents are recognized, cherished, and nurtured for the benefit of both the individual and the company. In a negative workplace, employees tend to wait passively for promotion or a pay raise. If they are passed over, they receive no explanation—and they do not seek one, despite their disappointment.

MEANINGFUL WORK, MEANINGFUL LIFE

As well as working in an optimistic environment, most of us find it important to do something that we find fulfilling. More than ever before, our work and studies help to define who we are, which means that spending eight hours a day doing work you dislike or that bores you or has no meaning for you is likely to make you generally unhappy and dissatisfied. In contrast, pursuing a course of study that challenges you and reflects your core values can be a source of great happiness, which radiates into all aspects of your life. According to a study by career counselor Sheila Henderson, people who are happy at work and school tend to have high levels of self-esteem and vitality and experience positive and productive relationships with other people.

In order to evaluate your career happiness and aspirations, you first need to explore your feelings toward your current academic path and extracurricular activities. Do you look forward to going to school most of the time? Do you feel that your studies will have a positive impact on others? Do you take pride in your education and derive satisfaction from it? If you had the opportunity, would you switch to a different course of study?

The purpose of this exercise is not to breed discontent where none previously existed. It may be that you are already on an academic path that you find meaningful and satisfying. However, if your answers to the above questions suggest that you are unhappy with your work, the optimistic approach is to take action. Ask yourself whether the problem lies with your conditions of education, or whether you find your profession intrinsically unfulfilling. In the former case, the solution might be to remain with the same course of study but transfer to a different school. However, if you think you are in the wrong course of study and this is making you unhappy, then you should seek a more fulfilling education.

Another option is to seek the guidance of your school counselor. An objective assessment of your personality type, your skills, and career options will help you to get organized and face the fear and uncertainty that you will inevitably experience. A good counselor will help you to weigh the risks and the rewards of changing your course of study so that your decision will be well informed. He or she will also be able to tell you what education, skills, and credentials you need to acquire in order to make a successful transition.

Doing some volunteer work or spending a week with someone who is working in the career that you are considering is a great way to gain some first-hand experience. Interview people who work in the field to find out what they like and don't like about the tasks they do. Read professional journals and magazines to get another view of the issues that you would have to deal with.

What you are looking for is your vocation—the activity that you are called to do, your life purpose. According to the psychologist Abraham Maslow, feeling that you are doing what you were meant to do in life and achieving your potential (he used the term "self-actualization") is at the pinnacle of human needs. Think in terms of two criteria: passion and contribution.

Take something that you are passionate about and use it to make a positive contribution to the world around you. Are you passionate about gardening? You could help people beautify their surroundings by designing gardens or you could set up community garden plots for families who live in high-rise apartment blocks. If you are not sure what you are passionate about, try focusing on something that you are good at. Ask your friends—if you are good at something, you probably take it for granted. Everyone has a gift and it is your responsibility to find out how your gift can be shared with others.

Once you know your life purpose, you will find and create meaningful work that is an extension of who you are and what you value. And you will face each day with the optimism that comes from a rich, fulfilling working life.

The ideas and techniques in this book will make a positive difference to your life, but only if you choose to put them into action. If you have been reading through the exercises, thinking "That sounds interesting, maybe I'll try it sometime," you need to go back to them and actually do them. "Sometime" never comes. Make a conscious commitment to become more optimistic by practicing your optimism skills daily so that they become second nature to you. Get into a routine: do the same exercise every day for a week, then switch to another exercise for the following week, and so on, until you build up a roster of positive thinking habits.

Another, crucial aspect of your routine is writing an entry in your optimism journal at the end of each day. Your journal is at the heart of your commitment to become an optimist. By comparing some of your early entries to your more recent ones, you can appreciate how much progress you have made, spurring you on to further achievements.

You should also use your relationships with other people to help you travel the path toward optimism. Learn from the way people you know overcome life's challenges. Recruit positive people to support you in your effort to stay on the sunny side of the street. The most important gift that you can bring to the world is your optimism. Everyone will benefit from your attitude: your family, your friends, your peers, and your community. If you want to change things in the world, you have to start by setting an example, by being positive and encouraging others to do the same. A positive mental attitude is not the preserve of a lucky few. You have a choice—choose to think well of yourself, choose to expect success, choose to endure, choose to be an optimist. When you choose optimism, nothing can stop you from creating the life that you want. When you choose optimism, you give yourself the key to good health, success, satisfying relationships, and a meaningful future. I urge you to make the study and practice of optimism a lifelong endeavor.